W. T. Horner

Horner's Buffalo and Niagara Falls Guide and Encyclopedia of Useful Knowledge

W. T. Horner

Horner's Buffalo and Niagara Falls Guide and Encyclopedia of Useful Knowledge

ISBN/EAN: 9783743442740

Manufactured in Europe, USA, Canada, Australia, Japa

Cover: Foto ©Andreas Hilbeck / pixelio.de

Manufactured and distributed by brebook publishing software (www.brebook.com)

W. T. Horner

Horner's Buffalo and Niagara Falls Guide and Encyclopedia of Useful Knowledge

BUFFALO AND NIAGARA FALLS

GUIDE

AND

ENCYCLOPEDIA OF USEFUL KNOWLEDGE.

CAREFULLY COMPILED.

W. T. HORNER, A. M., PUBLISHER,
PROPRIETOR BUFFALO JOURNAL AND RAILWAY GUIDE.
1874.

PREFACE.

It is with the most pleasing satisfaction that we present to the public the first edition of 10,000 copies of THE BUFFALO AND NIAGARA FALLS GUIDE AND ENCYCLOPEDIA OF USEFUL KNOWLEDGE. The advertising pages have been filled by the liberal and enterprising business firms of the city, although the effects of the late financial panic are everywhere visible. We have spared neither labor nor expense in making the GUIDE complete and reliable. The statistical data have been compiled from authentic sources and from books of reference possessed by the best libraries in the country; and thousands at a trifling expense can avail themselves of facts which otherwise would be beyond their reach. The entire work has been copyrighted and stereotyped, and regular editions of 10,000 copies will be published annually, with additional attractions of engravings of churches, public buildings and parks.

As the present edition seems inadequate from present appearances to supply the demand, we shall soon issue an extra edition of 5,000 copies. We wish to express our thanks to all our advertisers for their hearty co-operation in this enterprise, and we can assure our readers that they are numbered among the most reliable, enterprising and substantial business houses of Buffalo. Wishing all success and happiness,

I remain, with much respect, &c.,

THE PUBLISHER.

CITY OF BUFFALO.

Buffalo, "the Queen City of the Lakes," is a modern city in the most comprehensive sense. Her growth has kept pace with that liberal and progressive spirit which is the first cause of our national prosperity, and has done so much towards the advancement of that glorious civilization which builds up the desolate places and makes great cities rise where for ages "the tangled forest grew." And well does the Queen City merit her proud distinction, for she is indeed queen, by virtue of her position and influence, over the commerce of the five great lakes. Located at the mouth of Lake Erie, her vast grain elevators and storehouses are repositories for the products of the West, which ultimately find their way to the Eastern markets by the great water route, in which the Erie Canal is a connecting link between the Hudson River and the inland seas. The Queen City is also one of the most important coal marts in the country, having direct railroad connections with the coal-regions of Pennsylvania. Her manufacturing interests are large and steadily increasing, and her iron foundries, mills, and machine shops furnish employment to large numbers of industrious and skillful workmen. She has often been called "the Birmingham of America," and that she will justify the title, and be able to claim her undisputed right to it, there is no good reason to doubt.

During the war of 1812, the little village of Buffalo was burned by the British and their savage Indian allies. But it speedily rose from its ashes, and in a few years the foundations of the Queen City were laid. Even in those early days, Buffalo displayed much of that sturdy vitality and vigorous enterprise which has since been one of its prominent characteristics. In 1828 Buffalo was a village of 7,000 inhabitants; in 1832 its population was 15,000; 1835, 15,700; in 1840 it had reached 18,200; in 1845 to 30,200; in 1850 to 42,300; in 1855 to 74,200; in 1860 to 81,130; in 1865 to 94,000, and 1870 to 117,000. Buffalo must now contain a population of 161,782, an increase of 10,867 over 1872.

In 1872 there was received by lake over 62,000,000 bushels of grain and 30,000,000 by rail. To this may be added the receipts of lumber, live stock and other property, increasing greatly the amount of commerce of the city. Buffalo is rapidly becoming a railroad center. We have already the New York Central, the Erie, the Lake Shore & Michigan Southern, the Buffalo, New York & Philadelphia, the Grand Trunk, the Great Western, the Canada Southern, and the Buffalo & Jamestown. Buffalo has a magnificent school system, embracing the State Normal, in successful operation. We have magnificent County and City buildings in course of rapid erection, also a large edifice for a State Lunatic Asylum, also a magnificent Park and Boulevard system, which is being pushed to rapid completion. The suburbs of the city are constantly widening, and in the eastern part of the city especially, thousands of

WORLD'S DISPENSARY,

at Nos. 80, 82, 84 and 86 West Seneca Street, corner of Terrace, BUFFALO, N. Y., established for the cure of all **Chronic** (or lingering) **Diseases of either Sex**, particularly those of a **Delicate, Obscure, Complicated** or **Obstinate Character**, also for the skillful performance of all **Surgical Operations**, and as a headquarters for **Dr. Pierce's Family Medicines**, is the largest establishment of its kind in the world. It is organized with an eminent corps of Physicians and Surgeons, each devoting his whole time and attention to some particular branch of practice, by which the greatest skill is attained, while R. V. PIERCE, M. D., is the Physician and Surgeon-in-Chief, and is consulted in all important cases. Thousands of cases are annually treated, and each has the advantage of an educated and eminent **Council of Physicians**.

DR. PIERCE'S FAMILY MEDICINES.

If you would patronize Medicines, scientifically prepared by a skilled Physician and Chemist, use **Dr. Pierce's Family Medicines**. Golden Medical Discovery is nutritious, tonic, alterative, or blood cleansing, and an unequaled cough remedy; Pleasant Purgative Pellets, scarcely larger than mustard seed, constitute an agreeable and reliable physic; Favorite Prescription, a remedy for debilitated females; Extract of Smart-Weed, a magical remedy for pain, bowel complaints, and an unequaled liniment for both human and horse flesh; while his Dr. Sage's Catarrh Remedy is known the world over as the greatest specific for Catarrh and "Cold in the Head" ever given to the public.

R. V. PIERCE, M. D.,
PROPRIETOR, BUFFALO, N.Y.

new dwellings are going up, new streets are being laid out, and buildings intended for manufacturing and industrial purposes, have been erected. In the other suburbs, and in fact throughout the entire city, a healthy business progression is apparent, even to a casual observer.

Buffalo possesses a very salubrious climate, and in Summer, almost always, has the advantage of a cool and pleasant breeze from the lake, which sweeps through the broad streets, and exerts a grateful influence. The sanitary condition of the city is good, it has an excellent system of sewerage, and recent improvements bid fair to make up for any deficiencies that may have existed heretofore in regard to the water supply. The streets of the city are wide, well-paved, and many are beautified by shade trees. The number of elegant, palatial residences is large, and on Delaware avenue, Franklin, Niagara and other streets, may be seen some of the finest private dwellings in the State, many of which display remarkably fine taste and are triumphs of architectural skill. We write of the Buffalo of to-day, and shall endeavor, in the following pages, to point out briefly some of its most notable features.

THE PORT OF BUFFALO.

The marine interests of Buffalo are so extensive and so well understood, that a mere reference to them is all that is necessary at present. The port of Buffalo is a large and commodious one, protected by a strong breakwater, and admitting all kinds of lake craft, from the immense propellers of the Union Steamboat Company and the Western Transportation Company to the smallest schooners which ply between the upper lake ports and that of Buffalo during the season of navigation. Often during the summer, the entire harbor is crowded with all descriptions of vessels, and the scene is a very animated one. The amount of business done along the docks is immense, and large quantities of freight are transferred from vessels to the railroad cars. The New York Central Railroad and the Erie both have their freight-houses in close proximity to Buffalo River, and vessels are unloaded and their contents placed in cars with comparatively little delay. A large light-house stands on the extreme end of what is known as the old breakwater, and doubtless its warning signals have averted many accidents to vessels entering the port. The tug office is located at the foot of Main street, and the Custom House is in the Post Office building on the corner of Washington and Seneca streets.

On Central Wharf are the offices of commercial men, canal forwarders, elevator owners and commission merchants. The Board of Trade Rooms are also on Central Wharf, and there the gentlemen interested in maritime commerce "most do congregate." A very few figures will suffice to show what a heavy business is done:

During the year 1873, the number of vessels arriving at the port of Buffalo was 4,929, with an average tonnage of about 500 tons some, however, having a carrying capacity of 1,500 and 2,000 tons. The receipts of grain in bulk were equal to 104,032,135 bushels, against 91,354,000 bushels the previous year. Of course the receipts of coal and other products, both by lake and rail, were also very large. There are in all twenty-nine elevators with a capacity for holding 7,215,000 bushels of grain, and a transfer capacity of 2,715,000 bushels per day. These immense structures have been greatly improved of late, and in many of them the machinery is so constructed that railway cars and canal boats can be loaded at the same time vessels from Chicago, Milwaukee or Cleveland, as the case may be, are being unloaded. All are managed by an Elevating Association, composed of the city's prin-

GOWANS & CO'S

STEAM SOAP WORKS,

Nos. 269, 271, 273, 275, 277, 279 & 281 PERRY STREET,

Corner Chicago,

BUFFALO, N. Y.

SOLE MANUFACTURERS OF

THE CELEBRATED

MINERS' SOAP

Best in the World for general Family Use.

cipal merchants, and almost all the elevators are owned by Buffalo capitalists. They are indispensable to the city's commercial prosperity, and each one is a monument of individual enterprise. The grain elevators are a peculiar feature of Buffalo, which no stranger who visits the city should go away without seeing.

At different points along Buffalo river are extensive coal yards, lumber yards, stave factories, &c., and in each a thriving business is done.

THE BUFFALO PARK.

Buffalo can boast of one of the finest public parks in the country, both as regards extent, attractiveness and beautiful surroundings. It is well located in the north-westerly portion of the city, adjoining Forest Lawn Cemetery, and the principal drives can be reached either by Delaware avenue or Niagara street. The establishment of the Park was organized by an Act of the Legislature, passed April 14th, 1869, and since that time an immense amount of work has been done in the way of beautifying the grounds, laying out drives, planting trees, &c. The grounds, as selected by the Commissioners, cover, in the aggregate, some four hundred and ninety-five acres, one hundred and ten of which are located east of the extended line of Jefferson street. The name of "The Front" has been given to the grounds at the Fort Porter extremity, comprising about one hundred acres lying between Sixth street and the canal, and Vermont and York streets. In this area Fort Porter is located. It has long been a military station of the United States, and is now garrisoned by two companies of the First United States Infantry. The old stone fort was partially destroyed by fire some years ago, and has never been rebuilt. In its present state it resembles an ancient ruin. At this end of the Park is a magnificent view of Niagara river and the village of Fort Erie, on the Canadian side, with its dark background of woods. To the left, Lake Erie stretches away broadly into the distance, and the lake shore is visible for many miles. From "The Front," a parkway one hundred feet wide extends, following the broadened line of York street, and skirting the small Prospect Hill Parks, which are very attractive places of resort. From York street the parkway strikes across the junction of North and Rogers streets, where a circle of about six acres has been laid out. From this circle the parkway follows the line of Rogers street. At Bouck avenue we arrive at the westerly of two plazas, which have an area of about five acres each. From each of these plazas converging parkways extend to the central circle, mainly between Clinton and Bird avenues. From this circle the parkway extends, two hundred feet in width, to the Park proper, which covers about three hundred and twenty-five acres. Through this the Scajaquada Creek flows, and a beautiful artificial lake has been constructed at a central point. We make our exit from the main Park at its south-easterly extremity, by a parkway two hundred feet wide, which runs across Main street at the junction of Steele, a short distance north of the toll-gate, and sweeps in a noble curve through several pieces of wood till it skirts the easterly boundary of the Driving Park. The Park was laid out by the celebrated landscape architect, Mr. Frederick Law Olmsted, of New York.

The Buffalo Driving Park has long had the reputation of being one of the most famous trotting-parks in the world, and the annual meetings of the Association attract the best horses in the country. It was on this track that Dexter, Goldsmith Maid, American Girl and other "flyers" made some of their best recorded time.

Penrhyn Slate Company,

Manufacturers and Dealers in

ROOFING SLATE,

MARBLEIZED SLATE MANTELS, GRATES, FLOOR TILE, BILLIARD BEDS,

Blackboards, Wash Tubs, &c.,

Plain and Ornamental Slate Roofing.

OFFICE AND SALESROOM, } BUFFALO, N. Y.
304 MAIN STREET.

A. F. WATERS, Agent.

E. D. HOLMAN,

DEALER IN

Staple & Fancy Groceries,

(WHOLESALE AND RETAIL,)

TEAS AND COFFEES SPECIALTIES.

MANUFACTURER OF

Holman's Baking Powder.

293 MAIN STREET,

Between Swan and South Division Streets,

BUFFALO, N. Y.

THE PUBLIC SCHOOLS.

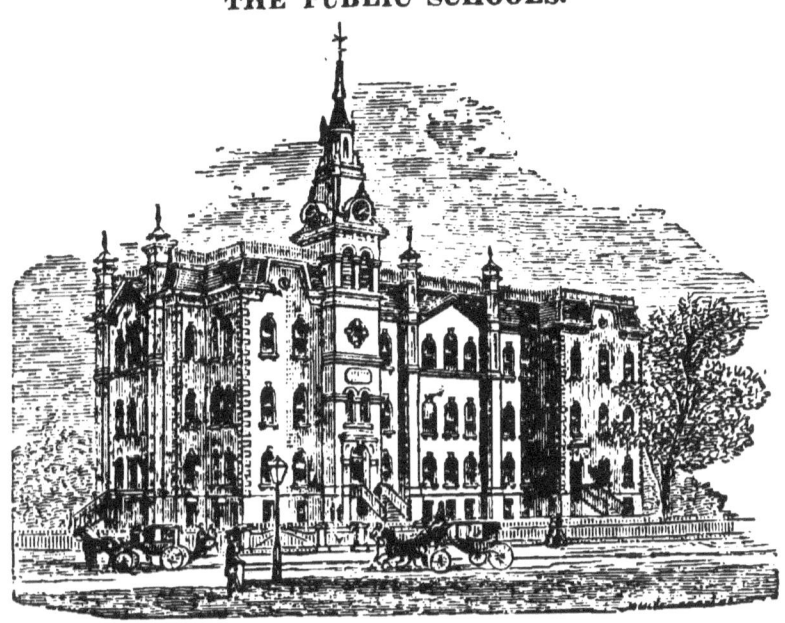

STATE NORMAL SCHOOL.

The city possesses thirty-six public schools, all of which are handsome, commodious buildings. There is also a Central or High School, and a State Normal School. The Central School is on Court street, near Niagara Square; and scholars enter this institution who have graduated from the District Schools. The course is a comprehensive one, continuing through three years. A graduate of the Buffalo Central School is the possessor of a most excellent education, and is well fitted to be a teacher or to occupy any position which requires thorough intellectual culture and practical knowledge. The State Normal School is located at the junction of Porter avenue, Jersey, Thirteenth and York streets. The land for its erection was given by the late Jesse Ketchum, familiarly known as "Father Ketchum," a man who did much for the public school system, and who, for many years, spent much of his time in visiting the schools and distributing presents to meritorious scholars. The corner-stone of the Normal School was laid April 15th, 1869, with imposing ceremonies. It is built of brick, in the Italian style, with a Mansard roof, and its dimensions in the clear are 164 by 86 feet. It has a tower fronting on Jersey street, and the entire structure is well proportioned and graceful in appearance. The first class graduated in July, 1873.

The Public Schools are under the general charge of a Superintendent of Education. The office is an elective one, and the term for which incumbents are chosen is two years. The present Superintendent is Wm. S. Rice, Esq., an experienced teacher and a gentleman of ability.

There are, in addition to the Public Schools, several private institutions of learning in the city, including the Buffalo Female Academy, the Heathcote School (Episcopal), and St. Joseph's College (Roman Catholic).

S. D. SIKES & BRO.,

Manufacturers and Wholesale Dealers in CANE SEAT and WOOD CHAIRS, No. 500 Clinton Street, BUFFALO, N. Y.

S. D. SIKES. *(Established 1859.)* EDWIN SIKES.

JOSEPH CHURCHYARD,

Lumber Dealer, Builder and General Contractor,

PROPRIETOR OF

Buffalo Planing Mill and Bellows Factory,

CLINTON ST., BET. ADAMS & WATSON STS., BUFFALO, N. Y.

MANUFACTURER OF

Sash, Blinds, Doors, Cisterns, Tanks, Stairs, Hand-Rails, Flooring, Siding, Ceiling, Mouldings, Mantels, Book Cases, Built up Hardwood Work, Newels, Curtain Cornices.

Scroll Sawing, Turning and Machine Work done.

Lumber of all kinds on hand, both rough and planed. Bills of Lumber sawed to order.

RAILROAD & FARM GATES, SNOW SHOVELS & SNOW FENCES.

BLACKSMITHS' & MOULDERS' BELLOWS.

CHARITABLE INSTITUTIONS.

The principal charitable institutions of the city are located as follows :
Buffalo General Hospital, High street.
Buffalo Orphan Asylum, Virginia street, below Delaware.
Church Home, Rhode Island street.
Home for the Friendless, corner of Maryland and Seventh streets.
Ingleside Home, No. 527 Seneca street.
Hospital of the Sisters of Charity, Main street, near Virginia.
Holly-Tree Soup House, Pearl street, near Seneca.

There are also a number of Catholic institutions which are exclusively denominational, and several benevolent societies, each of which does good work in its own peculiar field. Among those we have space to mention are the *St. George's Benevolent Society*, the *St. Andrew's Society*, the *Buffalo German Benevolent Society*, the *Firemen's Benevolent Association*, and the *Hebrew Union Benevolent Association*.

The Church Home is under the charge of an Episcopal society known as " The Church Charity Foundation," which covers a wide range of charities. A Home for aged and destitute women was opened in 1858, and an Orphan Ward added in 1866, when the present building of the Home on Rhode Island street was purchased.

The Buffalo Orphan Asylum was organized in 1835, and incorporated in 1837. It is under the supervision of a board of lady managers, chosen from the different churches.

The Ingleside Home was organized for the purpose of reclaiming fallen women, and under its auspices much good has been accomplished. It was incorporated in 1869.

The Home for the Friendless is for the benefit of destitute women, and such persons are admitted until places can be found for them in respectable families.

The Holly-Tree Soup House and Night Refuge is under the charge of a Committee of the Young Men's Christian Association. Meals are furnished the poor, and the night lodging-room is for the benefit of unfortunate but worthy persons, who would otherwise have to seek shelter at the station-houses.

ASSOCIATIONS, SOCIETIES, LIBRARIES, READING ROOMS, &c.

The *Young Men's Association* of Buffalo is an institution of a literary and scientific character, and occupies rooms in its own spacious building on the corner of Main and Eagle streets. It possesses an admirable library of about 27,000 volumes, comprising many rare and valuable works. The reading room is supplied with all the daily city newspapers, many from other principal cities, together with the best American and foreign quarterlies and monthly publications. It is open from 9 A. M. to 9 P. M., and is free to members of the Association and strangers introduced by members.

The *Young Men's Christian Association* has for its objects "the development of Christian character and activity in its members, the promotion of evangelical religion, the cultivation of Christian sympathy, and the improvement of the intellectual and spiritual condition of young men." Its library and reading rooms are over No. 319 Main street.

The *Mechanics' Institute of the City of Buffalo* was organized for "the mental improvement and culture of its members, the general

EAGLE IRON WORKS,
BUFFALO, N. Y.

ARCHITECTURAL IRON WORKS,

IRON STORE FRONTS AND GIRDERS,

Steam Engines and Boilers,

(Stationary and Portable)

TURBINE WATER WHEELS, MILL GEARING AND SHAFTING, MULEY AND CIRCULAR SAW MILLS, HOISTING MACHINES, &c., &c.

Office and Works, corner Perry and Mississippi Streets.

R. DUNBAR, SUP'T.

BROWN & McCUTCHEON,

Brass Foundry,

BRASS AND IRON FINISHING,

Copper, Tin and Sheet Iron Workers,
Agents for Huntoon's Patent Steam Governor,
Water and Steam Gauges,
Distillers' and Brewers' Work.

NOS. 16, 18 & 20 ELK ST.,

A. H. BROWN,
SAM'L M'CUTCHEON,
} **BUFFALO, N. Y.**

Manufacturers of Pumps, Hose, Hydrants and Stop Valves, all kinds of Brass Cocks, Globe Valves, Steam Whistles, &c. Jobbing promptly attended to.
CASH PAID FOR OLD COPPER AND BRASS.

promotion and advancement of mechanical interests, and the establishment of more intimate relations between employer and employee." Its rooms are in the American Block, Main street, and it has an extensive and valuable library. Since its organization in 1865, three "International Industrial Exhibitions" have been given under its auspices, with great success.

The *Grosvenor Library of Buffalo* was established through the liberality of one of its honored citizens, and is located over the Buffalo Savings Bank, on the corner of Washington and Batavia streets. The library is a very extensive and valuable one, and is free to all for purposes of reference. No books are allowed to be taken from the rooms. The leading magazines and periodicals are also to be found there, and the library is well worth a visit. It is an institution of which Buffalo may well be proud.

The *Buffalo Historical Society* occupies rooms in the Western Savings Bank building, on the corner of Main and Court streets, and its general design is to discover, procure and preserve whatever may relate to the history of Western New York, and the city of Buffalo in particular. It has a library of 4,477 volumes, and indexed pamphlets to the number of 4,430. It has a membership of over seven hundred. The Society possesses many rare and valuable curiosities, historic relics, portraits, and autographs of celebrities, &c.

The *Buffalo Fine Arts Academy* occupies rooms in the upper story of the Young Men's Association building, on the corner of Main and Eagle streets, and in its gallery may be found many works of art, including original paintings, copies from old masters, sculptures and casts from the antique, &c., &c. The object of the Academy is to "maintain a permanent gallery in Buffalo for the exhibition of Paintings and Sculptures, and to use such other means as may be desirable and efficient for the promotion and advancement of the same."

The *Buffalo Society of Natural Sciences* also occupies a portion of the Young Men's Association building, and possesses a very interesting museum of curiosities, daily open to the public, without charge. Some of the specimens on exhibition are very rare. The collection includes minerals, fossils, animals, fish, birds, &c. The Society also has a very valuable scientific library.

The *German Young Men's Association* was organized for the purpose of maintaining a library and reading room, and other means for promoting moral and intellectual improvement. It has a library of 5,000 volumes. The rooms are on the corner of Main and Mohawk streets.

The *Buffalo Law Library* is located in the third story of the Young Men's Association building, and the collection of legal works is a very valuable one.

The following is a list of the Singing Societies of the city:

The *Buffalo Choral Union;* meets at Goodell Hall, Johnson Place, Monday evenings.

Buffalo Liedertafel ; meets at Liedertafel Hall, Kremlin Block.

Orpheus Singing Society ; meets at Gerber Hall, 797 Main street.

Sængerbund Society ; meets at Turner's Hall, Ellicott street.

Buffalo Mænerchor.

The *Buffalo Club* occupies a large building on the corner of Delaware and Chippewa streets.

The *Forester Club* has rooms on Main street, above Eagle.

The *Audubon Club* (sporting) occupies rooms in the Arcade building.

The *Military Club* has rooms on Main street, opposite the Tifft House.

Have your Cleaning and Dyeing done at

THEBAUD BRO'S
FRENCH STEAM CLEANING AND DYEING
ESTABLISHMENT,

Office 16 South Division St. (near Main St).

BUFFALO, N. Y.

We have the largest and most complete establishment in the West. Gents' clothes cleaned in one to two days to give good satisfaction.

ALL ORDERS BY EXPRESS WILL RECEIVE PROMPT ATTENTION.

Established in 1868, and a complete success.

Buffalo Up-Town Crockery Store.

The Best place to buy

GLASS, CHINA,
CLOCKS,
PLATED WARE,

Fancy Goods, Etc.

GEO. E. NEWMAN,
444 Main St.

THE NEW CITY AND COUNTY HALL.

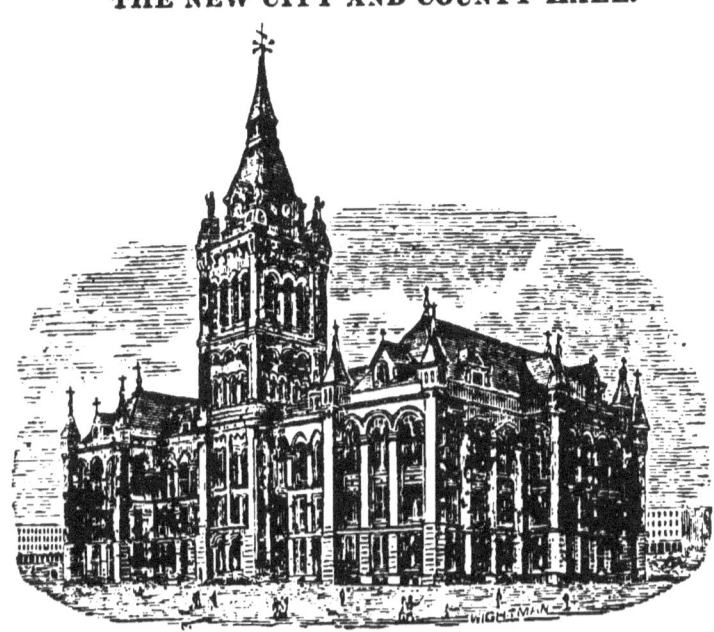

The new city and county buildings, now in process of erection, are located on Franklin Square, which is bounded by Franklin, Church, Delaware and Eagle streets. The corner-stone was laid, with imposing Masonic ceremonies, on the 24th of June, 1872. The stone used is the celebrated granite from Clark's Island, Maine, and the building will be fire-proof throughout. The style of architecture is that principally used in Italy during the middle ages, and termed the Lombardic, resembling the Norman. The structure is in the form of a double Roman cross, with bases adjoining, and extending longitudinally north and south. The body of the cross covers a space of 114 by 255 feet, the arms and heads each having 20 feet projection and 52 feet front. The tower will be 40 feet square at the base, and rise to a height of 245 feet.

The first story will be devoted to offices for city and county officials. In the second floor will be Court rooms, the Mayor's office, &c., and in the third, offices for the Park Commissioners, Superintendent of Education, and other officials; also the Common Council Chamber, and two Court rooms, with jury rooms adjoining. The basement will be used for storage purposes, and a section of it will be fitted up for the detention of criminals awaiting trial. The building, when completed, will present a very imposing appearance.

THE NEW STATE INSANE ASYLUM.

The corner-stone of the new Buffalo State Asylum for the Insane was laid by the Masonic order, on the 18th of September, 1872, Gov. Hoffman delivering the address on the occasion. The work of erection is now in favorable progress. The Asylum grounds are at North Buffalo,

BARNES, BANCROFT & CO.,
CASH AND ONE PRICE HOUSE,
260, 262, 264, 266 & 268 Main Street,
BUFFALO, N. Y.

The House of Barnes & Bancroft succeeded the old and very popular house of Sherman & Barnes in 1865. The Cash and One Price strictly adhered to increased our business so that in 1871 we moved into our spacious new store, where our sales now are over two millions annually. We believe there is no better evidence of the growth and prosperity of our city than the increase of our business, and we are gratified in knowing that a business built up on the "One Price and Cash System" has been a success.

BARNES, BANCROFT & CO.,

J. C. BARNES,
W. G. BANCROFT,
W. HENGERER.

260, 262, 264, 266 & 268 Main St.,
BUFFALO, N. Y.

and comprise 203 acres, bounded on the north by Scajaquada creek, on the south by Forest avenue, on the east by the line of Sherwood avenue, on the west by a line parallel to Grant street and 300 feet easterly therefrom—forming almost a complete square. The grounds have a frontage of 3,025½ feet on Forest avenue. The building is located as near the centre of the grounds as possible, and will consist of a large central or administration building, with ten wards arranged as wings on each side. The centre of the building is 1,600 feet east from the west line of the grounds, 1,425½ feet west from the east line, and 416 feet north of Forest avenue. The line of the west wing recedes from Forest avenue, until it stands 700 feet north and 500 feet east from the west line. The east wing recedes till the extent of the east building stands 1,200 feet north of Forest avenue, and 640 west of the east line.

The structure is of brown free-stone, roughly dressed, with the interior partitions of brick, and is designed to be fire-proof. Several small buildings are also to be erected on the grounds for the occupancy of those in charge. The location of the Asylum is an excellent one, with quiet, suburban surroundings. When finished, it will present a very fine architectural appearance.

THE BUFFALO WATER WORKS.

The Water Works of the city are located near the river, a short distance from the junction of Niagara and Seventh streets. The reservoir is bounded by Niagara, Vermont, Ninth and Connecticut streets. With the exception of the 25th and 26th days of December, 1872, and the 25th of January, 1873, when the water was below the inlet to the tunnel, owing to the prevalence of an easterly wind, the supply has always been equal to the demand, and with the present improvements at the works there is no reason to apprehend the recurrence of a water famine. A splendid engine, built at the Worthington Works, Brooklyn, now supplies the reservoir, and the engines formerly used are kept in readiness in case of an emergency. A new tunnel and inlet-pier are in course of construction, and during the year 1873 the old tunnel was thoroughly cleansed and its inlet lowered three feet, in order to effectually prevent a recurrence of the "east wind famine." When the improvements now under way are completed, the water will be taken from the river, a distance of 700 from Bird Island pier, and beyond the wash and roily water from Buffalo river. In case the openings in the new inlet-pier become closed by any cause, those of the old one can be immediately opened, and thus there will be in the future no lack of a supply of pure water. The Holly system is used in a northern district of the city, and its works are adjacent to the principal ones, as above located. The total number of fire hydrants now in use in the city is 746. During 1873 the average daily supply of water was 9,316,598 gallons. A scheme for building a new reservoir is now under consideration, but the plan has not been definitely settled.

The Water Works are under the management of a Commission, the Board being composed of three members. The office of the Commissioners and Superintendent of the Works is on West Swan street, near Main.

THE ERIE COUNTY ALMSHOUSE.

The "County House" is on Main street, beyond Forest Lawn Cemetery, and is a model institution of its kind. It has lately been designated a State Alms-House, under the new law relating to State paupers.

SENECA STREET, BUFFALO.

This rapidly improving thoroughfare extends from Erie street, east, to what is known as the Hydraulics. The large number of fine business blocks that have been erected in the past two or three years, and in course of erection, tend to confirm the belief that Seneca street will be the future leading wholesale street of the city. Among the many wholesale merchants may be found Smith, Lapham & Sawyer, wholesale Grocers; J. M. Henderson & Co., Proprietors Niagara Mills, Teas, Coffees and Spices; Joseph Guild & Sons, Proprietors Enterprise Mills, Teas, Coffees and Spices; Fowler & Son, wholesale Hardware.

At No. 133 Seneca street we come to the "*Buffalo Confectionery Works*," where are manufactured the celebrated "*Buffalo Candies*," so well and favorably known throughout the entire West. Messrs. Sibley & Holmwood, proprietors of the above concern, have, within the past twelve months, stepped to the very front rank of manufacturing confectioners. In looking over their stock of fine confections, we were very much surprised to see the large variety of candies (undoubtedly the largest assortment ever before offered in Buffalo). Their manufacturing department is in charge of one of the most careful workmen to be found in the United States. Some idea may be formed of the vast amount of candy manufactured by this house, when we say with *positive proof* that their sales from May 1st, 1873, to May 1st, 1874, *exceed* 300,000 lbs., which is strong evidence that dealers in the middle and western States second the efforts of Sibley & Holmwood to place none but strictly pure and wholesome goods on the market.

MILLINERY.

There are but few business streets in any city surpassing Main street, of Buffalo. The locality opposite the churches is both beautiful and business-like. The churches furnish an old and time-honored landmark. Among the oldest and most reliable business houses situated opposite the churches, the extensive wholesale and retail Millinery establishment of Wm. Wright stands pre-eminent. This house has had a most honorable record for fair dealing for many years, consequently its trade is increasing rapidly at home and abroad. In the wholesale department we find a large and extensive stock of the choicest and best goods. Looking at the history of this firm we find that the house was established in 1850 by Thomas Wright, and from 1860 to 1874 the business was carried on by James Wright; at present Wm. Wright is at the head of this house, and by his integrity and strict attention to business is gaining an enviable reputation and adding daily to his large list of customers.

Among other honorable firms located near this desirable centre of trade, we would name Wm. Woltge, dealer in Stoves, Ranges and House Furnishing Goods, and Harry Smith, Fashionable Hatter, both gentlemen of honor, honesty and strict business integrity.

THE ERIE COUNTY PENITENTIARY.

This institution is located on the corner of Fifth and Pennsylvania streets. Mr. Wm. Weston is Superintendent, and there is no better-managed penal prison in the country. The convicts, male and female, are employed in the manufacture of harness buckles, &c., for Messrs. Pratt & Letchworth, who pay the County of Erie for the work done. The Penitentiary has a chapel in which religious instruction is given every Sunday. The prison department of the place is well arranged, though greatly overcrowded, the number of inmates being generally between four and five hundred. The Penitentiary is built mainly of brick, and is surrounded by a high stone wall.

THE ERIE COUNTY JAIL.

The County Jail is on Clinton street, between the old and new Court-Houses, and is a dilapidated, old, stone building, entirely out of date and almost unfit for use. The cells are small and badly ventilated. The present jailer is Mr. Frank Nagle.

Several executions have taken place within the jail-yard, at different times, and hanging for murder is not "played out" in Buffalo. The two executions of most recent date are those of Patrick Morrissey and John Gaffney. The former was hanged on the 7th of September, 1872, for the murder of his own mother in the previous month of June; the latter on the 14th of February, 1873, for the murder of Patrick Fahey.

BUFFALO GENERAL HOSPITAL.

This hospital was erected and opened for the reception of patients in 1858. It is pleasantly situated at No. 100 High street. The building is 160 feet long, 50 feet wide and three stories high, with a capacity of 125 patients. Price per week, in wards, $5.00; in private rooms, from $7.00 to $14.00, with meals served in rooms, which are elegantly furnished. These prices include medical attendance, board, washing and ordinary nursing. The hospital is managed by a Board of Trustees, composed of the first men of the city. The present Superintendent is S. G. Johnson.

FOREST LAWN CEMETERY.

The "silent city" of Forest Lawn is beautifully located, adjacent to the public Park, and comprises about two hundred and seventy-five acres, well laid out, with broad carriage-ways and foot-paths. A creek runs through the grounds, and there is also an artificial lake. The firemen's monument, the Letchworth mausoleum, and numberless private monuments, are well worthy the attention of visitors. The Cemetery may be reached by the Main street cars, though the principal carriage entrance is on Delaware street. It is under the management of an Association, and the Secretary's office is on the corner of Main and Court streets, over the Erie County Savings Bank.

There is also a cemetery at Pine Hill, another at Limestone Hill (Catholic), and a burying-ground (the Potter's Field) on High street. All remains have recently been removed from old cemeteries on Delaware and North streets, in order to use the lands for building purposes.

THE POLICE FORCE.

The Buffalo City Police force is one of the best organized and most efficient in the country. Three Commissioners, one of whom is the

W. B. SIRRET & CO.

Manufacturers and Wholesale Dealers in

FURS, HATS, CAPS,

Straw Goods, Buffalo and Fancy Robes, &c.

No. 183 *Washington St.,*

W. B. SIRRET,
L. A. SIRRET,
ROBERT STAFFORD.
} *BUFFALO, N. Y.*

☞ *Buyers and Shippers of Raw Furs.*

SWEET, COOK & CO.

WHOLESALE DEALERS IN

Boots, Shoes & Rubbers

185 WASHINGTON STREET,

W. C. SWEET,
J. P. COOK,
GEO. W. SWEET.
} BUFFALO, N. Y.

Mayor of the city, compose the Board of Police, and the force consists of a Superintendent, Assistant, detective corps, eight captains, sixteen sergeants and about one hundred and sixty patrolmen, besides doormen and two special detectives in each precinct. The city is divided into eight precincts, and the headquarters are in the old Western Hotel building, on the corner of Pearl street and the Terrace. The offices of the Commissioners, Police Court, etc., are also in this building.

THE FIRE DEPARTMENT.

The Fire Department of the city combines the paid and volunteer systems, and is one of the most efficient in its workings that can be found in any city of the Union. The paid men have charge of the steamers, and the members of the hose and the hook and ladder companies are all volunteers. The Department is under the charge of a Superintendent, appointed by the Common Council. The system of fire-alarm telegraph is used, and the fire-bell is located on the tower adjacent to the City Buildings, on Franklin street. There are also gongs in the different hose and steamer houses and the Police Stations. Most of the steamers now in use are from the works of the Silsby Manufacturing Company, at Seneca Falls, N. Y.

MILITARY.

The Thirty-first Brigade N. G. S. N. Y., composed of the Seventy-fourth and Sixty-fifth Regiments, belongs exclusively to Buffalo. The headquarters of the former regiment are at the Armory, on North William street. Those of the Sixty-fifth are at the State Arsenal, on Batavia street. The city also possesses a splendid independent military organization known as "D" Co. Buffalo City Guard. The headquarters of the company are at the corner of Franklin and Eagle streets.

Two companies of the First U. S. Infantry garrison the government military station at Fort Porter. The headquarters of the regiment are in Detroit, Mich.

PLACES OF AMUSEMENT.

The *Academy of Music* (formerly the Metropolitan Theatre) is on Main street above Seneca, and is one of the most comfortable and well-arranged theatres in the country. The enterprising proprietors, Messrs. J. H. & H. L. Meech, have long held the confidence of the public by their able management, and understand just how to cater to the lovers and patrons of the drama. The Academy has an unsurpassed stock company, and the best actors and actresses of the day annually appear on its stage. It is worthy of note that the celebrated English novelist, Wilkie Collins, while staying in Buffalo, visited the Academy several times, and pronounced it one of the most charming places of entertainment in America.

St. James Hall is on the corner of Eagle and Washington streets, and is the property of the Young Men's Association; Mr. Charles G. Flint, lessee. It is adapted and used for all kinds of public entertainments, from a church fair to a minstrel performance, and from a society ball to a lyceum lecture.

The Opera House is in the Arcade building, on Main street, and the *Theatre Comique* on the Terrace, near Main street.

World's Prize Medals.

PEASE'S
IMPROVED OILS,

PRIZE MEDALS.

VIENNA, 1873.

LONDON,  PARIS,

1862. 1867.

American Institute, 1856--1867. Gold Medal, United States.
Gold Cross of Honor. Gold Medal of Progress.

Engine, Signal, Lard, Valve, Coach Oils,

"Premium Petroleum" and Head Light Oils,

Endorsed by experience and tests of years, and the highest authority
of the United States and Europe.

65 and 67 Main St., 82, 84 and 86 Washington St.,

BUFFALO, N. Y.

INTERNATIONAL BRIDGE AT BUFFALO, CROSSED BY THE GRAND TRUNK RAILWAY.

JOHN D. SMITH & CO.

Manufacturers OF Steam Heating APPARATUS

216 MAIN STREET.

SHACKLETON PATENT Generator AND RADIATOR.

Wrought Iron PIPE And Fittings

216 MAIN STREET.

BRASS GOODS FOR Water, Gas AND STEAM.

GAS FIXTURES, PLUMBING AND GAS FITTING.

J. S. LYTLE & SON,

MANUFACTURERS AND DEALERS IN

HARNESS,

GOOD ASSORTMENT ALWAYS ON HAND.

LADIES' AND GENT'S

Riding Saddles, Bridles, Whips, Lap Dusters, &c., &c.

HORSE FURNISHING GOODS,

20 EXCHANGE STREET,

(Opposite Mansion House.)

THE INTERNATIONAL BRIDGE.

The great International Railway Bridge, crossing the Niagara river between Black Rock (North Buffalo) and Fort Erie, and connecting the United States with the Dominion of Canada, was formally opened on the 3d of November, 1873. It was built under the auspices of a stock company composed of American and Canadian capitalists, and has been leased for twenty years to the different railroads crossing it, which are the Grand Trunk, Great Western, New York Central, Erie, Canada Southern, and New York, West Shore and Chicago. The bridge is about three-quarters of a mile long, including thirteen hundred feet of trestle-work over Squaw Island. In the main river are eight piers and two abutments; in Black Rock harbor, two piers and two abutments. The length of the superstructure in the main river is 1800 feet, in the harbor 450 feet. There are nine spans in the main river and three in the harbor, four of 190 feet in the clear and three of 240 feet in the clear. Over the main river are two draw openings of 160 feet each. In Black Rock harbor are two draw openings of 90 feet each, and one fixed span 220 feet long. The iron superstructure is that known as the "Pratt truss," and is very strong and durable. The entire bridge presents a very graceful appearance. A railroad track is laid over it, also a sidewalk for foot passengers. The bridge was built by Messrs. C. S. Gzowski & Co., of Toronto, and its estimated cost is $1,500,000.

THE RAILROAD DEPOTS.

The Railroad Depots of Buffalo are located as follows:

The Central Depot, on Exchange street, near Michigan.

The Erie Railway Depot, on the corner of Michigan and Exchange streets.

The Buffalo, New York & Philadelphia Railway Depot, at the corner of Exchange and Louisiana streets.

The Erie Street Depot, on Erie street, near the Canal bridge.

The Central and Erie freight depots are on Ohio street, and the freight house of the L. S. & M. S. R. R. on Louisiana street, below Exchange.

Trains of the New York Central and Lake Shore & Michigan Southern Railroads leave and arrive at the Central Depot. The latter road runs on Buffalo time, which is twenty minutes slower than New York time.

Trains of the B., N. Y. & P. and Buffalo & Jamestown Railways leave the depot of the former road, on the corner of Exchange and Louisiana streets, both running on Buffalo time.

The Erie Railway trains leave from the depot on the corner of Exchange and Michigan streets, on New York time.

Trains of the Great Western, Canada Southern and Grand Trunk Railroads leave from the Erie Street Depot, on New York time. Trains on the Lockport and Niagara Falls division of the Central Railroad also start from this depot.

THE STREET CARS.

Street cars run regularly on the following streets:

On Main street, between the dock and Cold Springs and Forest Lawn Cemetery.

On Niagara street, between Main and Amherst streets (Lower Black Rock).

On Genesee street, between Main and Jefferson streets.

On Exchange street, between Main and Louisiana streets (the Buffalo East-Side Street Railway).

THE AMERICAN BLOCK, BUFFALO.

By the kindness of Messrs. Adam & Meldrum, who own the engraving, we are enabled to present, on the opposite page, an accurate view of the large building known as the "American Block." It stands on the west side of Main street, between Eagle and Court streets, nearly opposite the Old Court House Park, and occupies the site of the old "American" Hotel, burnt down in 1865. On the first floor are six large stores, two of which, undivided, 160 feet deep by 50 feet wide, together with a basement of same size, the second floor 160 feet deep by 75 feet wide, and two large rooms on the third floor, are all occupied by the well-known firm of Adam & Meldrum. This firm began business here in 1867, occupying at first only a part of the first floor, 150 feet deep by 50 feet wide, and have been steadily growing out ever since; till it seems probable enough that one of these days they may occupy the entire American Block. By the excellent quality of their goods; by their very low prices; and by their strict adherence to their one price system, they have built up an immense trade, not only in Buffalo, but in the country all around. Visitors to Buffalo, and people who go there to do their trading, and large numbers from neighboring counties do so, should by all means go "Up-town" to the American Block, if only to see the fine building, the beautiful display of Dry Goods, and the crowds of people thronging the stores. The enterprise of this firm is sufficiently established by the fact that for two years they have been importing their foreign goods directly from the manufacturers in Europe. The advantage of this to the trade of Buffalo is apparent. The heavy expenses at New York Custom House are avoided, the profit of the New York importer is saved, and the purchaser in Buffalo reaps the benefit in cheaper goods. Of course it requires a business of magnificent proportions to dispose of goods in sufficient quantities to accomplish this. The direct importations of Adam & Meldrum during the present season will include invoices of Shawls, Dress Goods, Laces, Embroideries, Table Linens, Towels, Napkins, Bed Quilts, Table Covers, Lace Window Curtains, White Goods, Lace Shawls and Sacques, Woolen Cloths, and a large variety of Buttons and Dress Trimmings. Besides these they show full lines of all Domestic Manufactures, Cottons, Flannels, Cloths, &c., &c. The Carpet Room is on the second floor fronting on Main street, and contains a large stock of Carpetings of every grade and quality, from Hemp and Ingrain to Axminster and Moquette. In the basement, and on the second floor in the rear, are the Wholesale Rooms, where prompt cash buyers will find that they can assort their stocks of Domestics, general Dry Goods and Notions, at and at less than New York quotations.

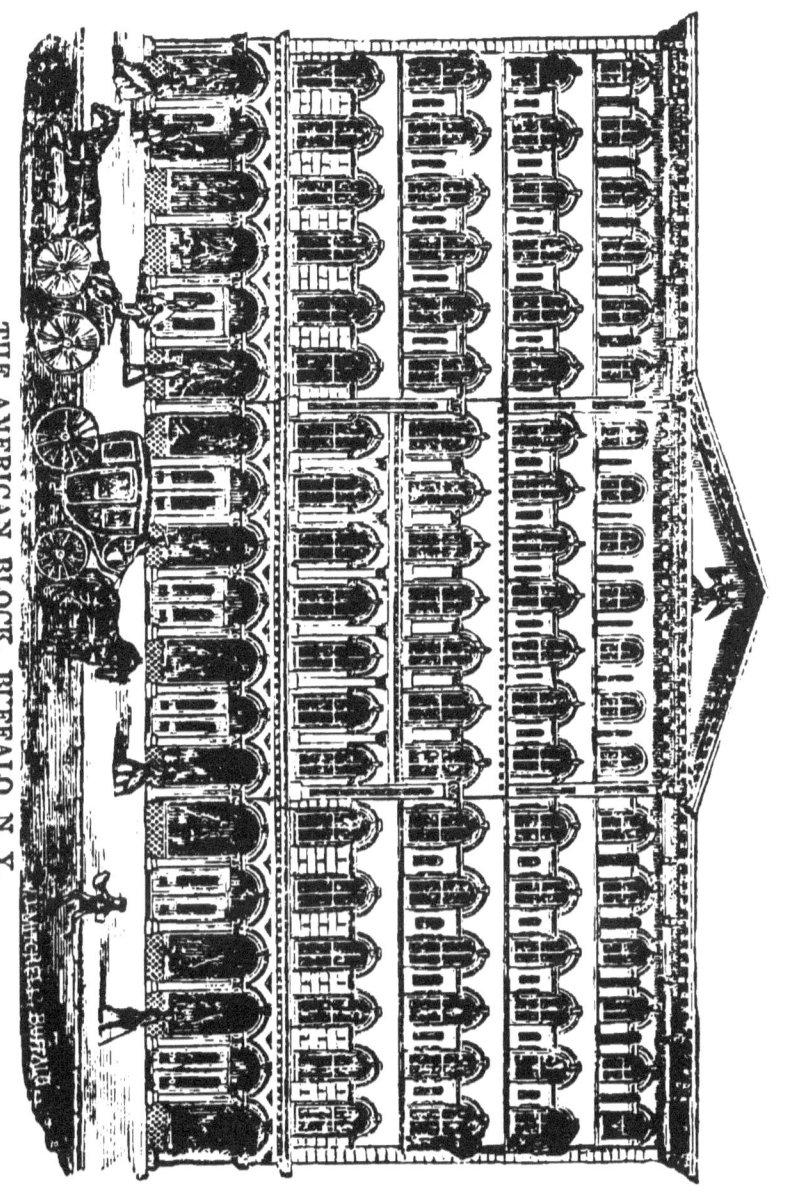

THE AMERICAN BLOCK, BUFFALO, N. Y.

SINGER SEWING MACHINE
AND
E. BUTTERICK & CO.'S PATTERN DEPOT.

In examining the different branches of business contained in the American Block, the extensive establishment of Mr. J. S. Dawley should by no means be overlooked, as the opportunity to observe a large and perfected business of this character should not be missed. Mr. Dawley's great experience in the Sewing Machine business, together with the fact that he has started with the right machine, has enabled him to completely control the business in this large city. By adopting a liberal, and at the same time conservative, policy in all dealings with his patrons, he has won the confidence of the public and transacted a large and profitable business. The Machines are here unpacked from their original cases, thoroughly tested by *steam power*, and before going into the hands of the purchaser receive most careful examination by competent and skillful machinists. By the results of long study and experience Mr. Dawley is enabled to sell this world-renowned Machine on most favorable terms, and in all cases fully warranted. Here also is to be found the best brands of Cotton and Linen Threads, Silk Twist, Oil, Needles, etc., etc. The justly celebrated E. Butterick & Co's Patterns for ladies' and children's garments are also sold at wholesale and retail. This business, first started in this city by Mr. Dawley, has grown into an extensive branch of trade, and people generally are beginning to appreciate the convenience and almost necessity of these patterns. For a small sum the perfect fitting pattern of *any* garment can be obtained, which contains full and explicit directions for purchasing the material, cutting and trimming, so that mistakes are an impossibility. Ladies' fine garments are also made to order, and with experienced operators are made in a superior and stylish manner. We recommend this veteran establishment to the examination and patronage of the public generally.

THE AMERICAN BLOCK.

The American Hotel was originally built in 1835-6 by Benjamin Rathbun for Alanson Palmer. The ground was that formerly occupied by stage yard and barns belonging to the late Bela D. Coe. The hotel was first opened in 1836 by Hodges & White. On Sunday morning, March 10, 1850, the hotel, together with a large amount of other property, was destroyed by fire, the flames having originated in what was then known as the "Globe Hotel," adjoining the American on the north. After the destruction of the hotel, the ground on which it stood —91 feet front—was purchased from Col. Bliss by John Michael. Mr. M. also purchased 45 feet adjoining, and re-erected the American Hotel. The new hotel was opened by Mr. Hodges on the 5th July, 1851, and remained under his proprietorship until burned, Jan. 25th, 1865, at 4.30 A. M. The fire was discovered on the premises occupied by Peter Diehl. The weather was intensely cold—a fearful storm was raging, its fury continually increasing. The hose was frozen to the ground and the steamers were covered with ice. It was determined by Mayor Fargo to take up a portion of the hose to the gas works and thaw it out and dry it.

The efforts of the fire department were of little avail in staying the progress of the fire, and it was determined to blow up the low brick buildings—the old Eagle Tavern Block—between the American and the four-story building owned by Mr. Bullymore. A keg of powder weighing 100 lbs. having been placed in position the explosion soon followed, and the time-honored "Eagle" was soon in ruins.

Calamitous as were the results of the conflagration, terrible as were the sufferings of those who, amid flame and storm, battled so manfully —all this was as nothing compared with the death of the three heroes, SIDWAY, GILLET AND TIFFT, members of Taylor Hose No. 1. In the discharge of their duty as firemen, regardless of their own safety, James H. Sidway, aged 25 years, Assistant Foreman of the Company; W. H. Gillet, aged 21, and G. H. Tifft, aged 24, true and faithful members of the same honored organization, lay buried beneath a fallen wall. In the absence of Chief Engineer French, First Assistant Engineer Spaulding assumed the command, and acquitted himself most creditably.

W. G. Fargo, then Mayor of the city, deserves mention for his extraordinary efforts at this great fire. His praise was in everybody's mouth. Early on the ground, he was the last to leave it. Quiet and energetic, calm, yet active, he was everywhere present to encourage and direct. The whole out-door force of the American and United States Express Companies and the Merchant's Dispatch be summoned to the aid of the sufferers.

The present American was built in 1865-6 on the same ground, and finished in the present magnificent style for stores and offices; and at present occupied by some of the most reliable and enterprising business and professional men of the city, many of whose names may be found in the Directory Department of this Guide.

BICKFORD, CURTISS & DEMING,

MANUFACTURERS OF BELT AND HOSE,

53 and 55 Exchange Street, Buffalo.

Messrs. Bickford, Curtiss & Deming, with twenty-five years' experience in the manufacture of Belt and Hose, and established in this city eight years, have built up an extensive business with all parts of the country. Their Belting goes directly to the consumer, who DEMANDS a PURE OAK AND SHORT LAP Belt and the very best that can be made, and their Hose to Fire Departments wishing the heaviest and best. Their Trade-Mark found above is placed on all of their Belt and Hose.

☞ We would advise those using the ordinary belting with long lap and of bogus oak, which is so apt to get out of shape and wear out in half the proper time, to try a belt in the worst places. We can assure our readers that the Belts of this old and well established firm will always give complete satisfaction.

WORLD-RENOWNED MANUFACTURING ESTABLISHMENTS.

Strangers stopping in the city could not entertain themselves more profitably than by visiting the following institutions, the pride of Buffalo:

KELLOGG BRIDGE CO.—Foot Hamburgh street.
UNION IRON WORKS—Foot Hamburgh street.
BUFFALO CAR CO.—Clinton street.
PRATT & CO.—Manufacturers Iron, Nails, &c., 44–50 Terrace.
PRATT & LETCHWORTH—Malleable Iron Works, 52–54 Terrace.
SIDNEY SHEPARD & CO.—Tinned and Wrought Iron French Hollow Ware 68 Main street.
F. S. PEASE—Manufacturer and dealer in Oils, 65 and 67 Main street. The proprietor is "King of Oil," having been repeatedly crowned by the autocrats of the Eastern hemisphere.
PRINCE & CO.—Melodeon factory, corner Maryland and Niagara st.
NOYE & SON—Mill Furnishing, 131 Washington street.
JEWETT & ROOT—Stove Works, Perry street, corner Mississippi.
MATTHEWS & WARREN—Railroad Bulletin Printing, Washington st.
STEAM FORGES—Niagara Steam Forge, Delany & Co., Perry street; Sizer & Williams, Steam Forge, Exchange street.
COAL INTEREST.—The trade in Coal for the Port is immense, and an inspection of the yards would afford interest to the stranger. The Directory department of the *Guide* will give their location.
LUMBER AND PLANING MILLS are first-class and should be inspected by the stranger and curiosity seeker. A vast amount of capital has been invested in this department, and Buffalo owes much of its prosperity to the enterprise of the men controlling these establishments.
All other business houses and manufacturers doing an honorable business and reflecting good credit upon the city as a great commercial centre, will be found in the Directory department of this *Guide*, alphabetically arranged. It may be relied upon as authoritative.

ELEVATORS.

The following Elevators are located on Buffalo Harbor: Bennett, City, Evans, Exchange, Hazard, Niagara, Tifft Fire-proof (formerly Plimpton), Reed, Richmond, Sternberg, Sturgis, C. J. Wells, Wilkeson, National Mills, Union, Brown, Coatsworth, Empire, Excelsior, Erie Basin, Fulton, Merchants, Marine, Swift Sure, Wadsworth, Wells, Williams, Watson.

BUFFALO CATTLE YARDS.

There are millions of money handled in the purchase of cattle yearly. A bank is about being established there to do the business. An omnibus for the cattle yards starts from the City Hotel, corner Exchange and Michigan streets, running, morning and afternoon, 4 times daily.

ESTIMATED VALUE OF RECEIPTS.

	1873.	1872.	1871.
Cattle	$26,889,056	$28,531,450	$34,586,460
Sheep	4,003,700	2,882,053	2,312,307
Hogs	16,625,000	14,501,090	10,632,168
	$47,517,753	$45,914,593	$47,560,935

BUFFALO MALLEABLE IRON WORKS,
PRATT & LETCHWORTH, Proprietors.

Near the terminus of the International Bridge on the American side, and directly opposite the Central Railroad Passenger Depot at Black Rock, are located the important Malleable Iron and Saddlery Hardware Works of Pratt & Letchworth. These are probably the most extensive Malleable Iron Works in the world, and give employment to a very large force of workmen. They are located on a tract of land some forty acres in extent, through the centre of which flows the Scajaquada Creek, affording ample and convenient facilities for receiving and shipping both raw material and manufactured goods. A branch of the New York & Erie Railroad also passes through the entire length of the grounds. The buildings are of great extent, the moulding room alone covering an area of 280 by 220 feet. Power is supplied by a 250 horsepower engine from the Fishkill Works on the Hudson. The engine room is a model of neatness, the floor, walls, and ceiling are finished in natural colored woods, and are in keeping with the elegant workmanship of the engine itself. Throughout the works the most improved appliances in moulding, casting, mallifying and finishing are brought into use, and no expense is spared to sustain the high reputation of the goods there manufactured. While the business partakes largely of the manufacture of Saddlery Hardware. Rings, Buckles, Bits, Trees, Hames, &c., it is by no means confined to this branch of industry alone, but embraces in its scope every conceivable variety of castings, from a knife handle to a steam engine, or from piano fixtures to threshing machines. The process of mallifying is simple, though it is one requiring great care and experience. The castings, if small, are cast from "gates," each mould or "gate" containing many duplicates of the same article connected together by a small band which easily breaks off with the touch of a hammer, the iron being exceedingly brittle before it passes through the annealing process. The castings are first carefully sorted, and all imperfect ones thrown aside; they are then placed in revolving cylinders, to remove the sand from the surface, after which they are tightly packed in iron vessels in layers of oxyde of iron—the scale which flies from iron in the process of rolling, and which has been allowed to oxydise or become rusted by exposure—and are then subjected to the intense heat of the furnaces for an average period of eight or ten days, according to circumstances. The combined action of the heat and the oxyde of iron produces the desired effect, rendering the iron tough and ductile, and after again passing through the revolving cylinders to brighten the surface they are ready for use. Tinning, Japanning, Nickel, as well as Silver, hand and Electro-plating are all carried on here.

The business store and offices of the firm are located on the Terrace. The former is an emporium of such a countless number of articles that it is impossible to enumerate them, suffice it to say that it embraces everything pertaining to the Saddlery Hardware business, and everything sold is, even when cheap, made of the best material and workmanship, no inferior goods whatever being allowed to pass from the works if known.

The business of this firm extends through New England and the entire West, from St. Paul to San Francisco and New Orleans, to the Canadas, and even to England, Mexico, South America and Australia.

BUFFALO MALLEABLE IRON WORKS.

PRATT & LETCHWORTH, - - Proprietors.

NATIONAL FLOUR MILLS.

CHOICE FAMILY FLOUR,
FARINA, RYE FLOUR, GRAHAM FLOUR,
CRACKED WHEAT.

Corn Meal and Feed of all kinds

For Sale at Lowest Market Prices, and Delivered to All Parts of the City.

ORDERS SOLICITED.

THORNTON & CHESTER,
Nos. 212, 214, 216, 218 and 220 Erie St.,

BUFFALO, N. Y.

PEERLESS FURNACE. Great Power of Heat, Purity of Air—Entirely Free from Gas.

J. B. PIERCE, 88 Seneca St., Buffalo.

Great Economy, Durability and Ease of Management.

EXTENSIVE MANUFACTURERS AND WHOLESALE DEALERS.

In addition to the extensive business establishments mentioned on a previous page, to be enumerated among the sound and substantial manufacturing institutions, adding much to the commercial importance of the Port of Buffalo, are the following:

DEALERS IN IRON OR BRASS MANUFACTURES.—James Brayley, cor. Carolina and Fourth, proprietor Pitts' Agricultural Works. Eagle Iron Works,—now furnishing castings for the New York City Post Office, —manufacturers of girders, the largest variety of building and architectural patterns west of New York City. R. L. Howard & Son, agricultural implements, Chicago street. Geo. L. Squires & Bro., Carroll st.; sugar mills shipped to Cuba and South America and other parts of the world. Niagara Bridge Works, connected with Pratt & Co., located at Black Rock. E. & B. Holmes, barrel machinery. Geo. W. Tifft, Sons & Co., engine builders. Also, Farrar & Trefts and David Bell, engine builders. Clark & Co., builders' hardware. F. D. Cummer, stationary engine builder. Francis Axe Co. and J. D. Shepard's Works, Chicago street. Bingham & Morgan, stoves. J. & N. C. Scoville, car wheels, Louisiana street. Jno. A. Seymour, chain factory, 663 Seneca street. Plumb, Burdict & Barnard, bolts. E. L. Hedstrom, iron. G. R. Wilson, iron. J. W. Ruger, cracker machinery, Perry & Chicago. Buffalo Scale Works, Exchange street. Drullard & Hayes, iron pipe works for gas and water. Frank & Co., pony planers, Terrace. Geo. Jones, safe builder, Terrace. Hubbell Bros. stoves. Thos. W. Toye, Hart, Ball & Hart and John D. Smith, plumbers. C. M. Horton, Pearl street, and D. C. Weed & Son, Main street, dealers in iron and hardware.

The most extensive white lead works are the Cornell Lead Works, cor. Delaware and Virginia streets. J. B Sweet & Son are extensive manufacturers of children's carriages. Slate roofing is extensively controlled by John Galt, yard located 126 Perry street, and the Penrhyn Slate Co., Main street. Among the soap manufacturers, R. W. Bell & Co., Gowans & Co. and Lautz Brothers supply the country for hundreds of miles both East and West. S. D. Sikes & Bro. control the trade in chairs. A. Best & Co., furniture. R. Ovens & Son and Geo. Mugridge & Son, bakers. Among the heavy dealers in lumber we would name Clarke, Holland & Co., E. & B. Holmes, Boller & Recktenwalt, Joseph Churchyard, and Dart & Brother. Morocco—Lymburner & Torry. Furniture—Herse & Co., Isaac D. White, Schlund & Doll. Weller, Brown & Mesmer. School Furniture—M. B. Chase. Flour Mills—National Mills, Thornton & Chester. Joel G. Garretson, manufacturer of light hardware. House Furnishing Goods—Heinz, Pierce & Munschauer, patent refrigerators, bird cages. Pianos—Ch. Kurtzman. Wholesale dealer in Medicine—Dr. Pierce. Frame Manufacturer—Mutter & Hoddick. Crockery—W. H. Glenny, Sons & Co. Coal—Longstreet & Co., Ellis Webster & Son. G. R. Wilson & Co., Anthracite Coal Association. Drugs—Harries, Powell & Co., Wm. Laverack & Co. Clothing—Altman & Co., Hofeller, Hochstetter & Strauss. Boots, Shoes and Rubbers—Sweet, Cook & Co., O. P. Ramsdell & Co. Hats, Caps and Furs—W. B. Sirret & Co., Bergtold Brothers. Dry Goods—Adam & Meldrum. Barnes, Bancroft & Co., L. H. Chester & Co. Hardware—Chas. E. Walbridge. Variety Store—Barnum & Son. Paper Hangings—M. H. Birge. Sewer and Drain Pipe—Charles H. Rathbun & Co. Dudley & Co. (oil, wholesale.) Gents' Furnishing Goods—H. Extein & Co. Refrigerators and Bird Cages—J. C. Jewett & Son. Confectionery—Henry Hearne. Cheese—Geo. W. Hayward.

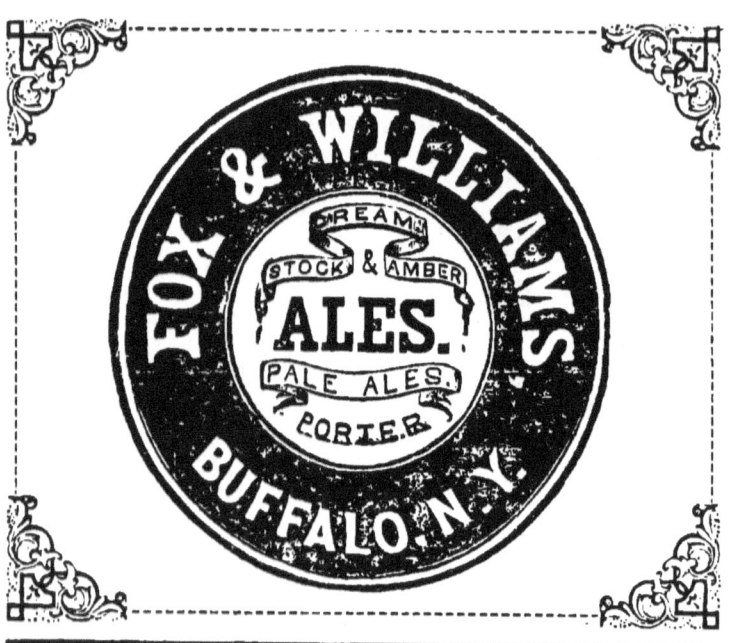

BOOTH, RIESTER & CO.

No. 29 Pearl Street, BUFFALO, N. Y.

JOHN C. POST,

WHOLESALE AND RETAIL DEALER IN

PAINTS, OILS, GLASS,

Artists' and Wax Flower Materials, &c. Importer of French and English Sheet and Plate Glass.

16 East Swan St. and 528 Seneca St., **BUFFALO, N. Y.**

☞ *GLAZING done to order.*

BUFFALO AND NIAGARA FALLS GUIDE. 37

THE INTERNATIONAL BRIDGE AT BUFFALO.

OFFICERS OF THE BRIDGE COMPANY.—*President*, C. J. Brydges, of Montreal; *Vice-President*, Hon. E. G. Spaulding, of Buffalo; *Secretary and Treasurer*, Joseph Hickson, of Montreal; *Counsel in Canada*, John Bell, of Belleville; *Counsel in the United States*, E. Carlton Sprague, of Buffalo; *Engineer*, E. P. Hannaford.

Directors.—C. J. Brydges, of Montreal; Hon. E. G. Spaulding, of Buffalo; Hon. James Ferrier, of Montreal; E. C. Sprague, of Buffalo; Aquila Walsh, of Simcoe, Ontario; P. R. Jarvis, of Stratford, Ontario; John Bell, of Belleville, Ontario.

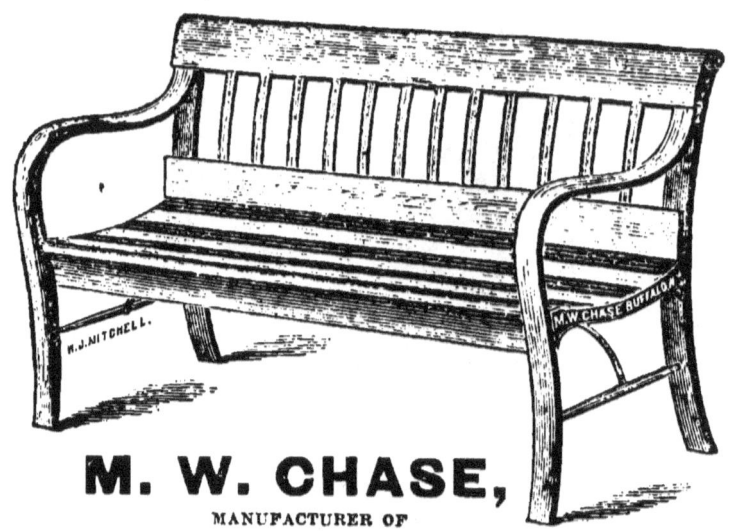

M. W. CHASE,
MANUFACTURER OF
CHURCH, HALL AND SCHOOL FURNITURE,
212 & 214 SEVENTH STREET, BUFFALO, N. Y.
Settees a Specialty. Send for Catalogue and Price List.

J. L. ALBERGER & CO.,
PORK PACKERS,
AND
Wholesale and Jobbing Dealers in Smoked Meats,
LARD, PORK, BEEF AND DRESSED HOGS,
OFFICE, 12 EXCHANGE STREET.
Hogs slaughtered on Commission. Packing House, corner Howard and Babcock streets.

ISAAC D. WHITE,
Manufacturer and Dealer in all kinds of
Parlor, Dining Room, Bed Room and Office
FURNITURE,
The Largest, Cheapest and Best Assortment,
AT WHOLESALE AND RETAIL,
257 MAIN ST., BUFFALO, N. Y.

THE CHURCHES.
PRESBYTERIAN.

First.—On the triangle bounded by Church, Niagara and Pearl sts.
Central.—Corner Genesee and Pearl streets.
Lafayette Street.—Lafayette street, between Main and Washington streets.
North.—Main street, between Chippewa and Huron streets.
Calvary.—East side Delaware Ave., between Chippewa and Tupper streets.
Westminster.—Delaware Ave., above North street.
Breckenridge Street.—Breckenridge street, near Niagara street, Black Rock.
East.—Seneca street, near Heacock street.
United.—Washington street, near Eagle street.
Wells Street Chapel.—Wells street, corner Carroll street.

METHODIST.

Grace.—Michigan street, between North Division and South Division streets.
Asbury.—Corner Pearl and Chippewa streets.
Delaware Avenue.—Corner Delaware Avenue and Tupper street.
Jersey Street.—Jersey street, corner Twelfth street.
Riverside.—Dearborn street, North Buffalo.
St. Mark's.—Elk street, near Alabama street.
Free Methodist.—Virginia street, corner Tenth street.
German.—Mortimer street, between Sycamore and Batavia streets.
Second German.—North Buffalo.
Bethel Mission.—On Perry street, near Washington street
Vine Street—(Colored).—Vine street.

BAPTIST.

Washington Street.—North-east corner Washington and Swan streets.
Cedar Street.—Corner Cedar and South Division streets.
Prospect Avenue.—Corner Prospect Avenue and Georgia street.
Prospect Chapel.—Corner Prospect Avenue and Rhode Island street. A branch of Prospect Avenue Church
Free Baptist.—Niagara Square.
First German.—Spruce street, north of Batavia street.
Second German.—Hickory street, near Genesee street.
Michigan Street—(Colored).—Michigan street, between Clinton and Batavia streets.

EPISCOPAL.

St. Paul's Cathedral.—On the triangle bounded by Erie, Church and Pearl streets.
Trinity.—Corner Mohawk and Washington streets.
St. John's.—Corner Swan and Washington streets.
Christ Church.—Delaware Avenue, between Tupper and Edward sts.
Ascension.—North street, at the head of Franklin street.
St. Luke's.—Niagara street, between Maryland and Hudson streets.
St. James'.—Corner Swan and Spring streets.
Grace.—Niagara street, corner Bidwell street.
St. Philip's—(Colored).—Elm street, between North and South Division streets.
St. Mary's.—Church Home, Rhode Island street.

UNITARIAN.

First Unitarian.—Corner Eagle and Franklin streets.

PORTER & WATKINS,
ARCHITECTS,

OFFICES: BUFFALO, N. Y., Townsend Block, corner of Main and Swan streets. ERIE, PA., Reed Block, corner of State and Seventh streets.

PLANS, SPECIFICATIONS, &c.,
Of Buildings of every description made to order.

ELEVATIONS, PERSPECTIVES AND DETAIL DRAWINGS

Promptly furnished for Churches, Public Buildings, City and Suburban Residences. Will Superintend the Erection of Work when desired.

JOHN GALT,
SLATE ROOFER

AND WHOLESALE DEALER IN

ROOFING SLATE.

Agent for Smith's Tubular Fluted Copper

Lightning Rods

The best protection against Lightning ever offered to the public, containing four times the surface and eight times the power of a ⅝ Galvanized Iron Rod.

126 Perry Street, Buffalo, N. Y.

UNIVERSALIST.

The Church of the Messiah,—Main street, near Huron street.

CATHOLIC.

St. Joseph's Cathedral.—Franklin street, near Swan street.
St. Michael's—(German).—Washington street, between Chippewa and Tupper streets.
St. Francis Xavier.—East street, near Amherst street.
St. Patrick's.—North Swan street, near Emslie street.
Holy Angels.—Prospect Hill, York street.
St. Joseph's Church.—Main street, near Eleyville Road, Buffalo Plains.
Holy Cross.—Cemetery, Limestone Hill.
St. Peter's—(French).—Corner Clinton and Washington streets.
Immaculate Conception.—Edward street, near Virginia street.
St. Mary's—(German).—Corner Batavia and Pine streets.
St. Louis—(German).—Main street, corner Edward street.
St. Bonifacius.—Mulberry street.
Mother of Sorrow.—Genesee street, near Herman street.
St. Bridget's.—Louisiana street, corner Fulton street.
St. Anne's.—Emslie street, near Lovejoy street.
St. Vincent De Paul's.—Main street, near Cold Springs.
St. John the Baptist's.—North Buffalo.

OTHER CHURCHES.

German Lutheran, Trinity.—Corner Maple and Goodell streets.
First German Lutheran, Trinity.—Michigan street, between Sycamore and Genesee streets.
Evangelical Lutheran, St. John's.—Hickory street, between Batavia and William streets.
German United St Paul's Evangelical.—Washington street, between Genesee and Chippewa streets.
Evangelical Association.—Corner Spruce and Sycamore streets.
German Evangelical, St. Peter's.—Genesee street, corner Hickory street.
United Evangelical, St. Stephen's.—Corner of Peckham and Adams streets.
Zion's Evangelical Reformed Church—(German).—Lemon street, near Cherry street.
Evangelical Association.—William street, corner Emslie street.
First French Protestant.—North-east corner Ellicott and Tupper sts.
Church of Christ.—Maryland street, near Cottage street.
High Street Mission and Benevolent Society.—Corner High and Mulberry streets.
Genesee Street Mission.—Jefferson street, between Batavia and Genesee streets.
German Evangelical.—Amherst street, North Buffalo.
Friends' Meeting-house.—173 Allen street.
Temple Beth-Zion.—Niagara street, near Franklin street.
Bethel Synagogue.—Pearl street, near Eagle street.

NEWSPAPERS AND PERIODICALS.

Buffalo Commercial Advertiser.—Daily, tri-weekly and weekly. Matthews & Warren, Publishers and Proprietors. Office, Commercial Advertiser Building, No. 253 Washington street, next the Post Office.
Buffalo Courier.—Daily and weekly. Warren, Johnson & Co., Publishers and Proprieters. Office No. 197 Main street.

BUFFALO, NEW YORK & PHILADELPHIA R'Y.

The Shortest and Best Passenger Route to the South-East and South.

In by-gone days travelers and tourists whose business or pleasure necessitated a trip between Buffalo, Philadelphia, Baltimore, Washington, or any of the Southern cities, dreaded the beginning of the journey, endured with forced resignation its manifold discomforts, and welcomed with joy its close.

Hardly a year has elapsed since the opening of the Buffalo, New York & Philadelphia Railway, but the changes wrought in that time have been little less than marvellous. This morning the traveler takes his seat in the luxurious Parlor Car almost within stone's throw of the foaming rapids of Niagara; to-night he sleeps in the Quaker City, or snugly ensconced in one of the comfortable hotels at Cape May is lulled to sleep by the roar of the breakers. This afternoon should business or pleasure call him southwards, the Pullman Sleeping Car rolls him out of the Buffalo depot after banking hours, lands him in Baltimore for breakfast, or at Washington before the day's business is fairly begun.

As a freight route the B., N. Y. & P. R'y has no superior. It materially shortens the distance between Buffalo and the Eastern and Southern cities; it has established a remarkably reasonable freight tariff, and as all goods entrusted to its agents are forwarded and delivered promptly, it is rapidly becoming the favorite line for all heavy shippers —coal, live stock, lumber, merchandise, etc.

MICHIGAN CENTRAL & GREAT WESTERN ROUTE.

The Michigan Central and Great Western are so regularly patronized by the commercial and mercantile portion of the traveling public, that, as far as these are concerned, it were needless for us to offer any remarks; but for the benefit of strangers and others, purposing to travel for pleasure or otherwise during the coming season, we will here recapitulate the improvements and additional facilities for travel now in operation on the above roads.

Four Express trains run each way daily between East and West, all of which run through or form close and direct connections between Chicago and New York in about thirty-six hours, affording a choice of two routes between Suspension Bridge or Buffalo and New York, as the trains of the Michigan Central & Great Western Railroad companies connect at those points with both the New York Central and the Erie Railroads. The Sleeping and Parlor Cars on these trains, also the first class coaches and baggage cars running through in connection therewith, are spacious and well ventilated, well furnished with every requisite for the comfort and convenience of travelers, and were built specially for this route. On the Atlantic and Pacific Express the celebrated Hotel Car accompanies the train between Chicago and Rochester, thus rendering unnecessary hurried meals at station dining rooms.

A large portion of the track has been doubled, and fast running, which would be impracticable on some roads, is rendered perfectly safe and pleasant to passengers on this route by the perfect state of track and rolling stock and the unrivalled efficiency of the station and telegraph service.

Buffalo Express.—Daily and weekly. Express Printing Company Publishers. Office No. 14 East Swan street.
Evening Post.—Daily. George J. Bryan, Publisher. Office No. 208 Washington street.
Buffalo Telegraph.—Daily and weekly. (German.) Fred. Geib, Publisher. Office Nos. 46 and 48 Batavia street.
Buffalo Demokrat.—Daily and weekly. (German.) Brunck and Held, Publishers. Office No. 509 Main street.
Buffalo Volksfreund.—Daily and weekly. (German.) Office No. 513 Main street.
Buffalo Freie Presse.—Daily and weekly. (German.) Reinecke, Zesch & Baltz, Publishers. Office No. 500 Main street.
Buffalo Christian Advocate.—Weekly. Ripley, Morse & Co., Publishers. Office No. 13 Brown's Building.
Buffalo Sunday News.—Weekly. Adams & Butler, Publishers. Office No. 200 Main street.
Buffalo Catholic Union.—Weekly. Catholic Publication Co., Publishers. Office No. 89 Main street.
The Globe.—Monthly. Globe Company, Publishers. Corner Main and Huron streets.
Our Record.—Monthly. Published by the Managers of the Home for the Friendless.
Our Young Men's Paper. Monthly. Published by the Young Men's Christian Association.
Live Stock, Farm and Fireside Journal.—Monthly. Published by the Buffalo Printing Co., No. 200 Main street.
The Journal.—Monthly. Devoted to Temperance and Literature. W. T. Horner, Publisher.
The Sunday Transcript.—Weekly. George Bro's & Co., Publishers. Office Nos. 192 and 194 Main street.
Buffalo Medical and Surgical Journal.—Monthly. J. F. Miner, M. D., Editor and Publisher. Office No. 61 South Division street.

SECRET SOCIETIES.

MASONIC LODGES.

Hiram, No. 105.—Meets on the second and fourth Fridays in each month, Main street, corner Swan street.
Concordia, No. 143.—Meets on the second and fourth Fridays in each month, Main street, corner Swan street.
Erie, No. 161.—Meets on the first and third Thursdays in each month, Main street, corner Swan street.
Washington, No. 240.—Meets on the second and fourth Thursdays in each month, Main street, corner Swan street.
Modestia, No. 340.—Meets on the first and third Tuesdays in each month, Main street, corner Swan street.
Queen City, No. 358.—Meets on the first and third Fridays in each month, Main street, corner Swan street.
The Ancient Landmarks, No. 441.—Meets on the first and third Thursdays in each month over Erie County Savings Bank, corner Main and Court streets.
Parish, No. 292 (Black Rock.)—Meets on the first and third Fridays in each month.
De Molay, No. 498.—Meets on the second and fourth Tuesdays in each month, corner Main and Swan streets.
Harmonie, No. 699.—Meets on the first and third Wednesdays in each month, over 416 and 418 Main street.

BERGTOLD & BROTHER,
WHOLESALE AND RETAIL,

HATS, CAPS & FURS,
291 MAIN ST., BUFFALO, N. Y.

Buffalo Chapter, No. 71, Royal Arch.—Meets on the first and third Wednesdays in each month, Main street, corner Swan street.
Keystone Chapter, No. 163, Royal Arch.—Meets on the first and third Tuesdays in each month, Main street, corner Swan street.
Adytum, No. 235, Royal Arch.—Meets on the second and fourth Wednesdays in each month, over Erie County Savings Bank, Main street, corner Court street.
Germania Chapter, No. 256, Royal Arch.—Meets on the first and third Thursdays in each month, over 416 and 418 Main street.
Buffalo Council, No 17.—Meets on the first Saturday in each month, Main street, corner Swan street.
Keystone Council, No. 20.—Meets on the third Saturday in each month, Main street, corner Swan street.
Lake Erie Commandery of Knight Templars, No. 20.—Meets on the first and third Mondays in each month, Main street, corner Swan street.
Hugh de Payen Commandery, No. 30.—Meets on the second and fourth Mondays in each month, Main street, corner Swan street.
Palmoni Lodge of Perfection, 14th degree A. A. R.—Meets on the second Saturday of each month, Main street, corner Swan street.
Palmoni Council of Princes of Jerusalem, 16th degree A. A. R.—Meets on the fourth Saturday of each month, Main street, corner Swan street.
Masonic Board of Relief.—Meets on the second Saturday in each month, Main street, corner Court street
Masonic Life Association of Western New York.
German Masonic Benevolent Association.

INDEPENDENT ORDER OF ODD FELLOWS.

Niagara Lodge, No. 25.—Meets every Monday evening at Odd Fellows Hall, Washington street, corner Seneca street.
Buffalo Lodge, No 37.—Meets every Tuesday evening, corner Seneca and Washington streets.
Walhalla Lodge, No. 91.—Meets every Thursday evening at German Odd Fellows Hall, corner Michigan and Cypress streets.
Odin Lodge, No. 178.—Meets every Monday evening, corner Michigan and Cypress streets.
Concordia Lodge, No. 187.—Meets every Friday evening, corner Michigan and Cypress streets.
German Bundes Lodge, No. 190.—Meets every Friday evening, corner Michigan and Cypress streets.
Oriental Lodge, No. 224.—Meets every Wednesday evening, corner Michigan and Cypress streets.
Red Jacket Lodge, No. 238.—Meets every Monday evening, over 416 Main street.
Erie Degree Lodge, No. 3.—Meets on the second and fourth Wednesdays in each month, corner Seneca and Washington streets.
Edda Degree Lodge, No. 33.—Meets on the first and third Tuesdays in each month, Cypress street, corner Michigan street.
Esther Degree Lodge, No. 3.—Meets on the first Thursday in each month.
Mount Vernon Encampment, No. 8.—Meets on the first and third Wednesdays in each month, corner Seneca and Washington streets.
Stuttgart Encampment, No. 70 (German).—Meets on the second and fourth Tuesdays in each month, Cypress street, corner Michigan street.
Erie District Grand Committee.—Meets quarterly.
Odd Fellows Benevolent Association.
German Odd Fellows Benevolent Association.

R. OVENS & SON,

Manufacturers of Aerated Bread, Crackers, &c.,

159, 161, 163, 165 & 167 Ellicott Street, Buffalo.

It must be seen by every reader of the City Guide that Buffalo is preeminently a manufacturing city. In this department it commands every element of success. Business men appreciate its unrivaled facilities for railroad and water transportation. Among the old and well established manufacturing houses of this city we take great pleasure in putting on record, the bakery establishment of R. Ovens & Son, as one of the largest and best conducted institutions in the United States; demonstrated by its baking capacity of 200 barrels of flour per day. Mr. Ovens, Senior, commenced the business in 1848, on Seneca street, and by establishing at the outset a high standard of bread, acquired a reputation for honesty, honor and integrity not only pleasing to himself, but worth a fortune to the firm he still represents. One of the maxims of the house is that good bread could not be made without good stock, competent bakers and a large supply of the purest water; all of which can be found upon the premises of this manufactory. In 1862 the business was carried on under the firm-name of R. Ovens & Son, and in 1866 the business increasing upon their hands compelled the firm to seek more commodious quarters on Ellicott street, in their present locality.

This firm is the sole manufacturers of Aerated Bread. Many other kinds of Bread, together with Crackers, Snapps, Jumbles, etc., are manufactured, and their shipments extend from Maine to Nebraska. To demonstrate the enterprise of R. Ovens & Son, we would state that the machine for baking crackers and cakes cost $10,000 and was imported from England; there are but four in the United States. The well for the supply of the water has been drilled into the rock and is sixty feet deep; making purer and better bread and crackers than can be furnished from the slimy water from Niagara river. Citizens of Buffalo do appreciate the enterprise of this firm, and it requires the carrying capacity of many wagons to supply the city with bread and crackers manufactured at this popular establishment. A large and commodious brick building is now being erected on the lot adjacent to the present site of the firm and will increase the capacity of the house considerably.

There are many other manufacturing establishments on Ellicott street, among which we would name the extensive furniture house of Hersee & Co. This firm has a most honorable record and is one of the oldest manufacturing institutions in the city.

KNIGHTS OF PYTHIAS.

Eagle Lodge, No. 69.—Meets every Friday evening, at "Red Jacket Lodge" room, over 416 Main street.
Triangle Lodge, No. 90 (German).—Meets every other Tuesday, at Kehr's Hall, Genesee street.

TEMPERANCE.
TEMPLE OF HONOR.

Royal Templars of Temperance.—Meets every Wednesday evening at Harmony Lodge Room, Main street, corner Eagle street.
Hiawatha Temple of Honor, No. 8.—Meets on the second and fourth Tuesdays of each month, over 416 Main street.

SONS AND DAUGHTERS OF TEMPERANCE.

Buffalo Division, No. 63.—Meets every Tuesday evening at 412 Main street.
Harvest Division, No. 113.—Meets every Friday evening at 412 Main street.

GOOD TEMPLARS.

Harmony Lodge, No. 516, I. O. G. T.—Meets every Tuesday evening, Y. M. A. Building, corner Main and Eagle streets.
Central Lodge, No. 573, I. O. G. T.—Meets every Thursday evening at 412 Main street.
Samaritan Lodge, No. 827, I. O. G. T.—Meets every Monday evening at 414 Main street.
Petra Lodge, No. 864, I. O. G. T.—Meets every Monday evening at Pratt Rolling Mills, Black Rock.
Olive Branch, No. 893, I. O. G. T.—Meets every Monday evening at 321 Vermont street.
Red Jacket Lodge, I. O. G. T.—Meets every Wednesday evening at 1260 Seneca street.
The Guards of Honor meet on the first Monday in each month at the Buffalo Female Academy.

AMERICAN PROTESTANT ASSOCIATION.

Excelsior Lodge, No. 11.—Hall, 414 Main street.
Eureka Lodge, No. 27.—Meets every Thursday, 414 Main street.

GRAND ARMY OF THE REPUBLIC.

Post Chapin, No. 2.—Meets at 414 Main street.
Post Bidwell, No. 9.—Meets at 414 Main street.
Post Wilkeson, No. 87.—Meets at Wilkeson Hall, 412 Main street.

A. PARDEE, *Pres.*   GUILFORD R. WILSON,   GEO. BEALS, *Treas.*
JAS. JENKINS, *Supt.*   *Vice-Pres.*   T. GUILFORD SMITH, *Sec.*

THE UNION IRON COMPANY,

MANUFACTURERS OF

Pig Iron, Bar Iron,

ROLLED SHAFTING & AXLES,

Girder Beams for Buildings and Bridges, Deck Beams for Boats,

ANGLE IRON, CHANNEL AND T IRON,

PLATE IRON, &c., &c.

Works, foot of Hamburg St.   **BUFFALO, N. Y.**

Albert Best & Co.

MANUFACTURERS OF

PARLOR FURNITURE FRAMES

AND

CENTER TABLES,

FOR THE TRADE.

BUFFALO, N. Y,

We have every facility for manufacturing first-class goods at the lowest rates, and our central location enables us to ship to all points, at very low rates of freight.

Price List and Catalogue furnished on application.

CITY AND COUNTY OFFICES.

The following gives the location of the principal City and County offices:

CITY.

Mayor.—On the corner of Franklin and Church streets.
Superintendents of Fire and Education.—Corner Franklin and Church streets.
City Clerk.—In the City Buildings, on Franklin street.
Comptroller.—City Buildings.
City Treasurer, Auditor, Assessors, and Engineer.—City Buildings.
Street Commissioner.—City Buildings.
Superintendent of Public Buildings.—City Buildings.
Common Council Chamber.—City Buildings.
Poormaster.—Police Building, on the Terrace.
Superior Court Judges' office.—Law Library, Y. M. A. Building.
Superior Court Clerk.—New Court House, Clinton street.

COUNTY.

Sheriff.—Old Court House, corner Washington and Clinton streets.
District Attorney.—Old Court House.
County Treasurer.—Corner of Pearl and Seneca streets.
Surrogate.—Corner Washington and Clinton streets.
County Clerk.—New Court House, Clinton street.
Supervisors' Room.—New Court House.
County Judge.—Y. M. A. Building.

GOVERNMENT OFFICES.

Custom House.—Post Office Building, corner Washington and Seneca streets.
Internal Revenue.—Post Office Building.
United States Court Room.—Post Office Building.
Clerk U. S. Court.—Post Office Building.
Deputy Marshals.—Post Office Building.

THE BANKS.

White's Bank of Buffalo.—Capital $200,000. Corner Main and Seneca streets.
Bank of Attica.—Capital $250,000. Corner Pearl and Seneca streets.
New York and Erie Bank.—Capital $300,000. Seneca street, between Main and Pearl streets.
Marine.—Capital $200,000. 112 Main street.
First National Bank of Buffalo.—Capital $250,000. Seneca street, between Main and Pearl streets.
Farmer's and Mechanic's National Bank.—Capital $200,000. Corner Main and Terrace streets.
Third National Bank of Buffalo.—Capital $250,000. Corner Main and Swan streets.
The Manufacturer's and Trader's Bank.—Capital $900,000. Seneca street, between Main and Pearl streets.
The German Bank of Buffalo.—Capital $100,000. Corner Main and Court streets.
Bank of Buffalo.—Capital $300,000. West side Main street, near Seneca street.
Buffalo Savings Bank.—Corner Washington and Lafayette streets.
Erie County Savings Bank.—Corner Main and Court streets.
Western Savings Bank.—Northwest corner Main and Court streets.
National Savings Bank.—Main street, near Erie street.
Bank of Commerce.—Main street, near the Terrace.

TIFFT HOUSE, BUFFALO, N. Y.

E. D. & H. TUTHILL, Proprietors.
The only first class house in the city.

HALL & SONS,

BUFFALO

Fire Brick Works,

AND

Tonawanda Common and Pressed Brick Works,

FIRE BRICK FOR ROLLING MILLS,

Forges, Blast Furnaces, Lime Kilns, Tanners' Ovens, Stoves, Ranges, &c.,

All manufactured of the best New Jersey clays, from our own mines.

Post Office Address, BUFFALO, N. Y.

SPORTING MEMORANDA.

[*Compiled from the New York Clipper, the standard sporting authority in America.*]

THE TURF—RUNNING.—¾ mile in 1:16, and one mile in 1:42¾, Alarm, at Saratoga, N. Y. 2 miles in 3:34½, Lyttleton, full weight, at Lexington, Ky. 3 miles in 5:27½, Norfolk, in California. 4 miles in 7:19¾, Lexington, 103lbs, at New Orleans. 50 miles in 1h. 52m. 31½ sec., actual riding time, by Chas. Reddiker, 10 horses, near Louisville, Ky. 200 miles in 8 hours, and 300 miles in 14h. 9m., by N. H. Mowry, at Bay View Park, San Francisco.

TROTTING.—1 mile in 2:16¾, Goldsmith Maid, in harness, at Boston. and Occident, at Sacramento, Cal. 1 mile in 2:18, Dexter, under saddle, at Buffalo, N. Y. 1 mile in 2:17¼, 2:19, 2:17¾ Goldsmith Maid, in harness, at Brooklyn—fastest three consecutive heats. 1 mile in 2:16¾, 2:18¾, Occident, at Sacramento, Cal.—fastest two consecutive heats. 1 mile in 2:15, 2:16, 2:19, Ethen Allen and running mate, against Dexter, Fashion Course, L. I. 1 mile in 2:24, Dexter, to wagon, and Lady Thorne, to wagon. 2 miles in 4:50½, Flora Temple, in harness. 2 miles in 4:56¼, Gen. Butler, 1st heat, to wagon, and Dexter, 2d heat, to wagon. 10 miles in 28:02½, John Stewart, to wagon, at Boston. 20 miles in 59:23, Capt. McGowan, in harness, at Boston. 50 miles in 3h. 55m. 40½sec., Ariel, in harness, 60lbs. driver. 100 miles in 8h. 55m. 53sec., Conqueror, in harness.

PACING.—1 mile in 2:14¼, Billy Boyce, under saddle, 3d heat. 1 mile in 2:17½, Pocahontas, to wagon. 3 miles in 7:44, Oneida Chief, under saddle.

PEDESTRIANISM—RUNNING.—70 yds. in 7¼ sec., by John W. Cozad, Fashion Course, L.I. 75 yds. in 7 sec., Wm. Bingham, Toronto. 100 yds. in 9¼ sec., by Geo. Seward, England. 500 yds. in 1:13, by James Nuttall, Manchester, Eng. 1 mile, level, in 4:17¼, W. Lang and W. Richards, dead heat, Manchester, Eng. 6 miles in 29:30, American Deer, London, Eng. 10 miles in 51:26, W. Lang, England; in 51:29, Deerfoot, England; in 51:34, American Deer, England. 41 miles in 4h. 18m. actual running time, Harry Howard, on a public road, England—including stoppages, 5hrs. 36min.

WALKING.—1 mile in 6:25, J. Stockwell, London. Eng.; same, 2 miles in 14:33, and 3 miles in 22:13½. 10 miles in 1h. 24m. 51¾sec., Howes, London, Eng.; in 1h. 31m. 19sec, Geo. Topley, Boston, Mass. 100 miles in 17½ hrs., exclusive of 1½ hours' rest, Capt. Barclay, Scotland. 400 miles in 6 days, W. Hughes, Boston, Mass. 1,000 miles in 1,000 consecutive hours, Capt. Barclay, Scotland, and J. Lambert, Boston, Mass.

OCEAN STEAMERS.—New York to Queenstown, in 7 days, 20 hrs. 21

ALLEN CHURCH,

WATCHMAKER AND JEWELER,

Agent for the Sale of Fine Watches,

No. 327 WASHINGTON ST.

BUFFALO, N. Y.

Particular attention given to Repairing Watches, Clocks and Jewelry of every description.

ALL WORK WARRANTED.

I make a Specialty of Fine Work.

GOOD NEWS!   GOOD NEWS!

THE BEST — **SIX-HOLE**

RANGE
IN THE WORLD.

J. B. PIERCE, Agent, 88 Seneca St., Buffalo.

SPORTING MEMORANDA.

min., City of Brussels; in 7 days, 22 hrs., Russia. New York to Liverpool, in 8 days, 14 hrs. 10 min., City of Brussels; in 8 days, 14 hrs. 45 min., Russia. Liverpool to New York, in 8 days, 21 hrs. 37 min., City of Paris. Liverpool to Australia, in 47 days, Golden Age.

RIVER STEAMERS.—26 miles in 1 hour, South America, on Hudson River. New York to Albany, 145 miles, in 6 hrs. 21 min., Alida; in 6 hrs. 51 min., nine landings, Daniel Drew. New Orleans to St. Louis. in 3 dys. 18 hrs. 14 min., R. E. Lee.

SAILING VESSELS.—New York to Liverpool, in 13 days, 1 hr. 25 min., Red Jacket. San Francisco to New York, in 80 days, Young America. Liverpool to Sydney, Australia, in 67 days, Patriarch.

RAILROADS.—10 miles in 8 min., Hamburgh to Buffalo, N. Y. 14 miles in 11 min., locomotive and six cars, N. Y. Central road. 18 miles in 15 min., Paddington to Slough, England. 81 miles in 82 min., special train, Rochester to Syracuse, N. Y. 91 miles in 90 min., actual running time, special train, Janesville to Chicago, Ill. 305 miles in 7 hrs. and 32 min., Albany to Niagara, N. Y.

JUMPING—MAN.—Standing, 13ft. 5¾ in., Ed. Searles, Utica. Running, 29 ft. 7 in., John Howard, Chester, England.

HORSE.—39 ft., over water, Chandler, Warwick, Eng. 34 ft., over hurdles, Calverthorpe, Eng. 33 ft., over wall, Lottery, Liverpool, Eng.

LIFTING—HARNESS.—3,300lbs., W. B. Curtis, New York; 2,900lbs., Dr. Winship, Boston. HAND.—1,230lbs., W. B. Curtis, New York; 1,000lbs., Dr. Winship, Boston.

SKATING.—1 mile in 1 min. 56 sec., Wm. Clarke, Madison, Wis. 30 miles in 1 hour, George Seward, England. 30 hours' skated, with 30 minutes' rest, by Miss Annie C. Jagerisky, aged 17, at Detroit, Mich.

TYPE-SETTING.—George Arensberg set 2,064 ems, solid minion, —one breakline to each stickful,—in one hour, New York.

BRICKLAYING.—W. D. Cozzens laid 702 bricks in 12 minutes, Philadelphia.

BILLIARDS —John McDevitt made a run of 1,483, four-ball game, in a match with Goldthwaite; he subsequently ran 1,458 in a match with Joseph Dion, Chicago, Ill. Maurice Daly ran 153, three-ball game, at Chicago tournament, 1873.

PRIZE RING.—Longest battle on record—6 hrs. 15 min., James Kelly and James Smith, Australia. Longest in England—6 hrs. 3 min., Mike Madden and Bill Hayes. Longest in America—4 hrs. 20 min., Fitzpatrick and O'Neil, Maine. Shortest battles on record.— 2 minutes by Watson and Anderson in England, and by Kelly and Parkinson in America.

RATTING.—25 rats killed in 1:28, by Jacko, London, Eng; same, 100 in 5:28; 1,000 in less than 100 min.

DIRECTORY

OF LEADING AND RESPONSIBLE

BUSINESS HOUSES AND PROFESSIONAL MEN OF BUFFALO, N. Y.

Agencies.

Mercantile—R. G. Dun & Co., Washington Block.
Improved Mercantile—J. M. Bradstreet & Son, Washington Block.
Commercial—John McKillop & Co., Nos. 7 to 10 Brown's Buildings.

Ales.

Fox & Williams, see page 36.

Architects.

Oatman, F. W., American Block.
Porter & Watkins, Townsend Block, see page 40.

Attorneys.

Park, Charles H., No. 190 Main street.

Auction and Commission.

Irish, C. G., No. 303 Washington street. Sales Wednesday and Saturday mornings.

Booksellers, Publishers and Stationers.

M. Taylor, wholesale and retail dealer, No. 263 Main.

Awnings, Flags, Tents, Sails.

Provoost, D., & Sons, foot Lloyd street.

Bakeries.

Mugridge, George, & Sons, manufacturers of Soda Biscuit, Butter Crackers, Patent Bread, Snaps, Nos. 10 to 14 Elk street.
Dies, Charles, No. 52 East Seneca street, dealer in Bread, Confectionery, and Pastry.
R. Ovens & Son, Nos. 165 and 167 Ellicott street, see page 46.

Bird Cages.

Heinz, Pierce & Munschauer, Nos. 52 to 58 Mechanic street.

Boots and Shoes.

Chamot, C. P. (Theatrical a specialty.) No. 269 Washington street.
Garner, G., & Son, No. 19 South Division street. Special attention to construction of foot.
Wolter, H. G., Gentlemen's Custom Work, No. 15 W. Eagle.
Sweet, Cook & Co., No. 185 Washington street, see page 20.
Towers, T., No. 394 Main street, see page 70.

Book and Job Printing.

Eby, P., Nos. 409 and 411 Main street, corner Clinton. English and German.

Book Binding and Blank Book Manufactories.

Chichester, J. L., Washington street, see third page of cover.

Bork, W. H. & Co., Nos. 255 to 259 Washington street.

Buffalo Fertilizing Company.

Alexander & Archer, Bone Super-phosphate Lawn Fertilizers. Plant Food for Plants and Flowers. Office, Nos. 297 and 301 Michigan street; Works, Babcock street, East Buffalo.

Builders' Hardware.

Shepard, John D. Foundry, and manufacturer of Small Iron Castings. No. 126 Chicago street.

Carriages.

Chamberlain & Joyce, manufacturers of. Repository, Pearl street; Works, corner Mohawk and Pearl streets.

Harvey & Wallace, a large assortment of fine Carriages of our own manufacture. Nos. 104 and 108 Terrace.

Children's Carriages.

Sweet, J. B. & Son, manufacturers of, Nos. 297, 299 and 301 Niagara street.

Cloak and Dress Making.

Mr. & Mrs. Constantine, No. 321 Main street. Work executed at short notice.

Clothing Houses.

Altman & Co. (wholesale), Nos. 226 and 228 Washington street.

Meyer, T., The One Price Clothier (retail), No. 404 American Block.

Confectionery.

Sibley & Holmwood. No. 133 Seneca street. The leading Confectioners of Buffalo. Sell more goods than any other confectionery house in the city. See page 18.

Hearne, Henry, No. 110 Seneca street. The largest and cheapest manufacturing confectioner in Western New York.

Barker, C. B., successor to John Benson & Son, No. 157 Main st. The oldest and largest confectionery establishment in State of New York.

Albert Ey, No. 301 Main street, wholesale dealer in American and French Confectionery.

Bullock's Celebrated Chocolate Creams and Maple Sugar Caramels of different flavors made fresh daily. Ice cream and refreshment restaurant, Exchange street, corner Washington street.

Mayer's, No. 336 Main street. Parties and families supplied with all kinds of Creams, Ices, Jellies, Chocolate, Russe, etc.

Coal.

Hedstrom, E. L. & Co., Miners and Shippers, No. 29 Seneca street.

Longstreet, S. P. & Co., No. 20 East Seneca street, see fourth page of cover.

California Beer and Mineral Water.

Adams & Co., No. 43 Carroll street, manufacturers and dealers in California Beer and Mineral Water. Wholesale dealers in Champagne Cider and Cider Vinegar. Physicians pronounce the Beer a healthy tonic.

Chair Factory.

Sikes, S. D. & Bro., No. 500 Clinton street, see page 10.

Coal Hods and Coal Vases.

Heinz, Pierce & Munschauer, Nos. 54 to 58 Mechanic street.

Copper, Tin and Sheet Iron.

Kast & Co., Nos. 15, 17, 19 Scott street. Malt House Work.

Cracker Machinery.

Ruger, J. W. & Co., corner Perry and Chicago streets.

Crockery.

Newman, G. E., No. 444 Main street, see page 14.

Dentistry.

Phillips, T. S., No. 476 Main street, opposite Tifft House. Teeth extracted without pain.

Drain and Sewer Pipe.

Rathbun, Charles H. & Co., manufacturers of and dealers in Drain and Sewer Pipe, No. 12 Henry street.

Dress Making.

Mme. Valentine, No. 440 Main street. A good fitting guaranteed.

Dry Goods and Carpets.

Adam & Meldrum, Nos. 396 to 402 Main street. See page 26.

Barnes, Bancroft & Co., Nos. 200 to 208 Main street. See page 16.

Chester, L. H. & Co., importers and dealers in Dry Goods, Carpets, Upholstery and House Furnishing Goods. The best, the choicest and completest assortment in each department. No. 259 Main street.

Flint & Kent, No. 261 Main street. Ladies' Underwear a specialty.

Druggists.

Champlin, O. H. P., No. 75 E. Seneca st. Sign of Big Mortar. Dealer in purest drugs, and manufac'r of Talbot Health Bitters. Try a bottle.

Thompson's. The Druggist and Chemist, No. 17 Court street, between Main and Pearl.

Drugs, Groceries, Paints, etc.

Laverack, W. & Co., No. 230 Washington street.

Dyeing.

Thebaud Bros., office No. 16 South Division street, see page 14.

Edge Tools.

White, L. & I. J., wholesale manufacturer of.

Engravers.

Juengling, H. F., No. 293 Washington street, manufacturing Jeweler. Door Plates and Seals a specialty.

Engines and Boilers.

Tifft, G. W., Sons & Co., manufacturers of Steam Engines, Boilers and Architectural Castings, Nos. 25 and 27 Washington street.

Cummers, F. D., Nos. 47, 49 and 51 Water street.

Farrar & Trefts, Nos. 54 to 66 Perry street. See page 64.

Fine Arts, Pictures and Frames.

Fay & Hubbell, dealers in Paintings, Engravings and Chromos, No. 403 Main street.

Benson, D. D., No. 258 Main street. Fine exhibition of Paintings and Works of Art. French Plate Mirrors a specialty.

Fire Brick.

Hall & Sons, office at Pratt & Co's, Terrace. See page 50.

File Works.

Eagle File Works, Nos. 274 to 278 Court street. See page 70.

Forging (De Laney Forge and Iron Co.)

Car Axles, Shafting, Wrought Iron Work, No. 306 Perry street.

Florists.

Long Bros., general wholesale and retail FLORISTS, Nurserymen, Seedsmen. City Depot No. 440 Main street. Park Greenhouse and Flower Gardens front on Park. Nursery at Williamsville, N. Y. Shipping of all kinds of Floral Designs for Weddings, Funerals, etc. Plants and seeds made a specialty. Catalogue free to any address.

Flour Mills.

National Flour Mills, Nos. 212 to 220 Erie street. See page 74.

Foundries.

Eagle Iron Works, corner Perry and Mississippi streets. See page 12.

Brown & McCutcheon (Brass), Nos. 16 to 20 Elk street. See page 12.

Frames and Mouldings.

Hinze, Bunting & Co., Picture Frames, Looking Glasses and Bulletin Boards, No. 331 Main street.

Simonds, H. L., No. 15 South Division street. Frames made to order; terms reasonable.

Frame and Moulding Factory.

Mutter & Hoddick, Nos. 25 to 31 Washington street.

Furniture.

Hersee & Co., Nos. 247 to 255 Ellicott street

Schlund & Doll, No. 472 Main street.

Persch & Gessert, Furniture and Upholstery Warerooms, Nos. 52 and 54 Genesee street.

White, Isaac D., No. 257 Main street. See page 38.

Best, Albert & Co., Perry street. See page 48.

Groceries.
Beard & Thyng, Nos. 263 and 265 Washington street (Fancy Fruits).
Holman, E. D., No. 293 Main street. See page 8.
Scott, Geo. W., No. 17 East Seneca street. See second page of cover.
Bartholomy, Peter, No. 289 Main street. See third page of cover.

Gun Powder.
Laflin & Rand Powder Co., No. 231 Washington street.
Oriental Powder Mills, A. B. Young, Ag't, 42 Exchange st. See p. 87.

Hair Goods. (Human.)
Mme. Thayer, No. 479 Main street. The only reliable Hair Emporium.

Harness.
Lytle, J. S. & Son, No. 20 Exchange street. See page 24.

Hardware and Iron.
Pratt & Co., Terrace Square.
Pratt & Letchworth, Terrace Square.
Horton, C. M., corner Pearl and Seneca streets.
Walbridge, C. E., Nos. 297, 299 and 301 Washington street.
Garretson, J. G., manufacturer of Window Locks; also, Ink wells for School Furniture, No. 45 Henry street.

Hats, Caps and Furs.
Sirret, W. B. & Co., Washington street. See page 20.
Smith, Harry, Fashionable Hatter, No. 327 Main street.
Bergtold & Brother, No. 291 Main street. See page 44.

House Furnishing Goods.
Heinz, Pierce & Munschauer, Nos. 52 to 58 Mechanic street.

Hotels.
Tifft House, Main street. See page 50.

Insurance.
Mutual Insurance Co. of Buffalo, capital $100,000. Insures Buildings, Merchandise, Household Furniture and other property against loss or damage. Office, No. 459 Washington street. M. Leo Ritt, Secretary; John Langner, Vice-President; John P. Einsfield, President.
Stevens, W. C., General Agent North American Insurance Company, of New York, No. 381 Main street.

Iron.
Hedstrom, E. L. & Co., importers and dealers in, No. 29 Seneca street.
The Union Iron Company, foot of Hamburgh street. See page 48.
Drullard & Hayes, No. 344 Exchange street. See page 64.
Weed, D. W. C. & Co., No. 284 Main street. See page 72.

Leather Belting and Hose.
Bickford, Curtiss & Deming, Nos. 53 & 55 Exchange st. See page 30.

Kellogg Bridge Company.
Works, foot of Hamburgh street. See page 66.

Livery and Boarding Stables.
Bidwell's, Nos. 409, 411 and 413 Niagara street. See page 87.

Marbleized Slate and Mantel Manufacturing Co.
Williams Bros., No. 156 Virginia street; store room, No. 20 W. Eagle.

Medicines.
Dr. R. V. Pierce, Nos. 80 to 86 West Seneca, cor. Terrace. See page 4.

Merchant Tailors.
Stuart, W. H., No. 17 Court street.
Schneider, J., No. 323 Washington street.
Sippel, G., No. 35 East Seneca street. Finest of stock.
Haffa, J. G., No. 325 Washington street.

Millinery Goods.
Wright, William, No. 325 Main street, opposite churches. See page 18.

Milk Dealers.
Erie Co. Milk Association, No. 32 Ellicott street. The purest milk.

Mill Stones and Mill Machinery.
Noye, John T. & Son, Washington street.

Men's Furnishing Goods.
Exstein, Hiram, & Co., No. 187 Washington street.

Music Store.
Cottier & Denton, No. 269 Main street. Pianos and Organs for sale.

News Depots, Books and Stationery.
Hawks, T. S., No. 31 East Seneca street, opposite the Post Office.
Buckland, G. W., No. 16 East Seneca street. Hawks' old stand.

Nurseries.
Zimmerman, G. & Sons, No. 571 Main street.

Oil.
Pease, F. S., Nos. 65 and 67 Main street. See page 22.

Opticians.
Andrews, R. E., No. 294 Main street. Optical, Mathematical and Physical Instruments.

Paints, Oils and Glass.
Post, John C., No. 16 East Swan st. and 528 Seneca st. See page 36.

Paper Hangings and Window Shades.
Burley, E., No. 46 Niagara street. Latest styles and lowest prices.
Birge, M. H., No. 218 Main street, wholesale dealer in Paper Hangings, Curtains and Oil Cloths.

Pickles, Sauces, &c.
Bell Bros., manufacturing and wholesale dealers, Nos. 10 to 14 Pearl st.

Planing Mills.
Holmes, E. & B., corner Washington street and Erie Canal.
Churchyard, Joseph, Clinton street. See page 10.
Clarke, Holland & Co., corner Court and Wilkeson sts. See page 68.

Plumbing.
Smith, John D. & Co., No. 216 Main street. See page 24.

Physicians.
Colton, H. E., northeast corner Mohawk and Washington streets.
Lewis, Dr. G. W., (Homœopathic), Pearl street, near Court street.

Provisions.
Bullymore, Richard, wholesale and retail, Michigan street.

Paper Collars.
Davis & Waldron, manufacturers of and wholesale dealers in Paper Collars and Gent's Furnishing Goods, No. 7 W. Seneca street.

Photographers.
Knight's Gallery, Main street, cor. Erie. First class Photographs.
Farnsworth & Phelps, No. 381 Main st. Crayon Portraits a specialty.

Pork Packers.
Alberger, J. L., & Co., No. 12 Exchange street. See page 38.

Powder.
Oriental Powder Mills, A. B. Young, Ag't, 42 Exchange st. See p. 87.

Real Estate and Insurance.
Hume & Sanford, No. 16 W. Swan street.

Refrigerators, Filters, Coolers and Bird Cages.
Jewett, John C. & Son, manufacturers of, Washington street.
Heinz, Pierce & Munschauer, Nos. 52 to 58 Mechanic street.
Vogt, P. A., No. 31 Main street and No. 482 Washington street.

Rubber Goods.
Goodyear Rubber Emporium, E. A. Rockwood, proprietor, No. 242 Main st. Belting Hose, Packing, Boots, Shoes, and everything made of rubber at manufacturers' prices. Satisfaction guaranteed.

Roofing.
Penrhyn Slate Co., office No. 304 Main street. See page 8.
Galt, J., No. 126 Perry street. See page 40.

Saw Mills.
Pierce, Jerome & Co. Bill Timber sawed to order. No. 414 Louisiana street.

Scales.
Fairbanks Scales of every variety and for all uses for sale, No. 93 Main.

Sewing Machines.

Singer, J. S. Dawley, No. 402 Main street. See page 28.
American Sewing Machine, No. 8 East Huron street. Try them..

Shingle Mills.

Pierce, Jerome & Co., manufacturers of Cut and Sawed Pine Shingles, No. 414 Louisiana street.

Soap.

Thompson, H., manufacturer of Staple Soap, Nos. 270 to 280 Perry street, corner Exchange street.
Gowans & Co., Steam Soap Works, Nos. 269 to 281 Perry street, corner Chicago. See page 6.
Bell, R. W. & Co., Washington street. See outside cover.

Stained Glass.

Booth, Riester & Co., No. 29 Pearl street. See page 36.

School Furniture.

Chase, M. W., Nos. 212 and 214 Seventh street. See page 38.

Stoves and Ranges.

Woltge, W., No. 319 Main street. See page 70.
Pierce, J. B., No. 88 Seneca street. See page 52.

Stamping Works.

Shepard, Sidney, & Co., No. 68 Main street. See page 79.

Stoves and House Furnishing Goods.

Perrine & Strawn, No. 133 Main st. Best Portable Range in market.

Street and Sewer Contractor.

McConnell, D. W., Nos. 89 and 91 Franklin street.

Seedsmen and Millers.

Harvey Bros., wholesale and retail, No. 262 Washington street.

Stove Polish.

National Stove Polish Co., No. 74 Pearl street.

Teas, Coffees and Spices.

Hayward, Geo. W., Buffalo Steam Coffee and Spice Mills. Dealer and shipper in New York Cheese, Butter and Dried Fruits, Nos. 305 and 307 Washington street.
Excelsior Mills, corner Main and Hanover streets, P. J. Ferris.
Joseph Guild & Sons, Enterprise Mills, No. 86 Seneca street.

Undertaking.

Sackett, J. B., No. 174 Pearl street, next to Skating Rink.

Wagons.

Chamberlain & Joyce, cor. Pearl and Mohawk sts. Examine our $140 wagon.

Washing Crystal.

Shirrell & Co., Nos. 72 and 74 Pearl street.

Watches, Clocks and Jewelry.

Stevens Bros., Tifft House Block, Watches, Clocks, Jewelry, Bronzes, Solid Sterling Silver Ware, Silver Plated Ware, American and Swiss Gold and Silver Watches. Ladies' and Gentlemen's Watch Chains, Ladies' Necklaces and Lockets.

Castle, D. B., No. 161 Main street, dealer in Gold and Silver Watches.

Schaefer, C. A., No. 11 Court street, dealer in Gold and Silver Watches. Jewelry repairing a specialty.

Pleuthner, A., No. 600 Main street, dealer in Gold and Silver Watches.

Church, Allen, No. 327 Washington street. See page 52.

Water Coolers.

Heinz, Pierce & Munschauer, Nos. 52 to 58 Mechanic street.

White Lead and Lead Pipe.

Cornell Lead Co., corner Virginia and Delaware streets. See page 83.

Wire Works. (Wholesale and 'ail.'

Scheeler & Baer, No. 7 Lloyd street.

Dow's Wire Works, No. 517 Washington street. Bank and Office Work a specialty.

Wood Engraving.

Lowe, John C., Nos. 198 and 200 Main street. Mechanical Engraving a specialty.

Wightman, C. D., Designer and Engraver on Wood. Makes a specialty of all work entrusted to his care, and aims to do it in No. 1 style, in the Arcade, Room No. 30.

EDITORIAL NOTICE.

In future editions the Directory Department will be increased until every reliable and enterprising firm in Buffalo will be found correctly classified. Many first class houses have been necessarily omitted in this edition.

Hotels at Niagara Falls.

Clifton House, Canada side.
Cataract House, American side.
International House, American side.
Spencer House, American side.

NIAGARA FALLS.

AMONG the wonders of the world may justly be classed the Falls of Niagara. They are the pride of America, and their grandeur, magnitude, and magnificence are well known to all the civilized world. Millions have flocked thither from all countries to gaze with feelings of the deepest solemnity on the tumultuous fall of waters, and to revere the power and majesty of the Creator as these are set forth and realized amid the sublime scenery of this stupendous waterfall.

In the following pages we shall attempt to guide the traveler to the various points whence the finest views of the Falls may be obtained, and, thereafter, conduct him to the spots of peculiar interest in their neighborhood.

The great lakes of North America—Superior, Michigan, Huron, and Erie—pour the flood of their accumulated waters into Lake Ontario through a channel of about 36 miles in length. This channel is named the Niagara River, and is part of the boundary between Canada and the State of New York. Twenty-two miles below its commencement at Lake Erie occur the famous Falls of Niagara. These Falls are divided into two by Iris or Goat Island. The American Falls are 900 feet wide, by 164 feet high. The Horse-Shoe or Canadian Fall is 2000 feet wide, and 158 feet high. The origin of the name is uncertain, but it is supposed to be of Iroqnois extraction, and to signify the "Thunder of Waters." The roar of the Falls is sometimes heard at a great distance, but of course it is constantly modified by the direction and strength of the wind. Over this magnificent precipice the irresistible tide rushes at the rate of 100 million tons of water every hour! It is computed that the precipice is worn away by the friction of the water at the rate of about one foot a year, and it is believed that the Falls have gradually receded from Queenston, seven miles below, to their present position. The river above the Falls is studded with islands of all sizes, amounting to 37 in number. The width of the stream varies from several hundred yards to three miles. At the Falls it is about three-quarters of a mile wide. The total descent from Lake Erie to Ontario is 334 feet. So much for statistics.

The Falls of Niagara were first seen by a white man nearly two hundred years ago. *Father Hennepin*, a French Jesuit missionary, first saw them when on an expedition of discovery in the year 1678.

The spots of interest to be visited, besides the great Fall itself, are:—The ground where the memorable battle of Lundy's Lane was fought; the Whirlpool below the Falls; the Suspension Bridges; the Devil's Hole and the Bloody Run; the Queenston Heights, General Brock's Monument; Burning Spring, &c.

DRULLARD & HAYES,

FOUNDERS OF

CAST IRON PIPE,

FOR

WATER & GAS,

No. 344 Exchange Street,

SOLOMON DRULLARD, }
GEO. B. HAYES.   BUFFALO, N. Y.

FARRAR & TREFTS,

MANUFACTURERS OF

STEAM ENGINES, BOILERS

AND MACHINERY,

54 to 66 Perry Street, - BUFFALO, N. Y.

PROPELLER WHEELS A SPECIALTY.

ALL KINDS OF REPAIR WORK SOLICITED.

The *Village of the Falls*, through which you pass on your way from the cars, lies on the east side of the river, in the immediate vicinity of the grand cataract, 22 miles by rail from the city of Buffalo on Lake Erie, and 300 by rail from Albany. Being a fashionable place of resort during Summer and Autumn, *the Hotels* at this village are excellent in all respects, and most agreeable abodes for those who intend to sojourn for a time within sound of the Falls. The chief of them are the *Cataract House*, the *International Hotel*, *Spencer House* (opposite Depôt); three magnificent houses, in which every comfort is combined with elegance. The Cataract House is situated at the head of Main street, overlooking the American Rapids. From the parlors of this famous hotel a fine view is had of the Rapids, Goat Island, the Bridge, and the Canada shores, considered among the principal features of Niagara. Conveyances may be had from any of the above hotels to all parts of Niagara. Moving forward down the street leading past the hotels just mentioned, we come into full view of the river at the point where it is spanned by the

Cast-iron Bridge Over the Rapids.

Here the first perceptions of power and grandeur begin to awaken in our minds. The noble river is seen hurrying on towards its final leap; and, as we stand upon the bridge looking down upon the gushing flood of water, that seems as if it would sweep away our frail standing-ground and hurl us over the dread precipice whose rounded edge is but a few yards further down, we begin, though feebly as yet, to realize the immensity of this far-famed cataract. This is the finest point of view from which to observe the *Rapids above the Falls*. The fall of the river from the head of the rapids (a mile above the Falls) to the edge of the precipice is nearly 60 feet.

At the other end of the bridge is *Bath Island*, connected with *Iris* or *Goat Island* by another bridge; and beyond Goat Island there are a few scattered rocks, which are connected with it by means of a third bridge. These rocks lie on the very brink of the precipice, between the *American* Falls and the *Horse-Shoe* Fall, and on them stood a tower named the *Terrapin Tower*, which commanded a magnificent view of Niagara. This tower has lately been removed, having been pronounced unsafe. But there are finer points of view than this. Moreover, we shall afterwards have to conduct our reader to various points of great interest on and around these Islands, which, however, no one will feel disposed to visit until he has given his undivided attention to the wonderful Falls from the most striking points of view. We therefore recommend him not to cross over to Goat Island in the first instance, but, after having stood upon the bridge over the rapids above described, retrace his steps and hasten down the banks of the river a few hundred yards, to a spot named *Point View*.

Before proceeding thither, however, we may say a word or two in reference to the bridge we are about to leave. The elegant and substantial structure that now spans the river at this point, was erected by the Messrs. Porter, the proprietors of Goat Island. It is made of iron, on the plan of Whipple's iron-arched bridge, and is 360 feet long, having 4 arches of 90 feet span each. The width is 27 feet, embracing a double carriage-way of 16½ feet, and two foot-paths of 5¼ feet each, with iron railings. All of the materials used in its construction are of the best quality, and the strength of all the parts is much beyond what is considered necessary.

Visitors may cross and recross this bridge as often as they wish for 50 cents per day, or for one dollar for the whole season.

KELLOGG BRIDGE CO.
OF BUFFALO, N. Y.

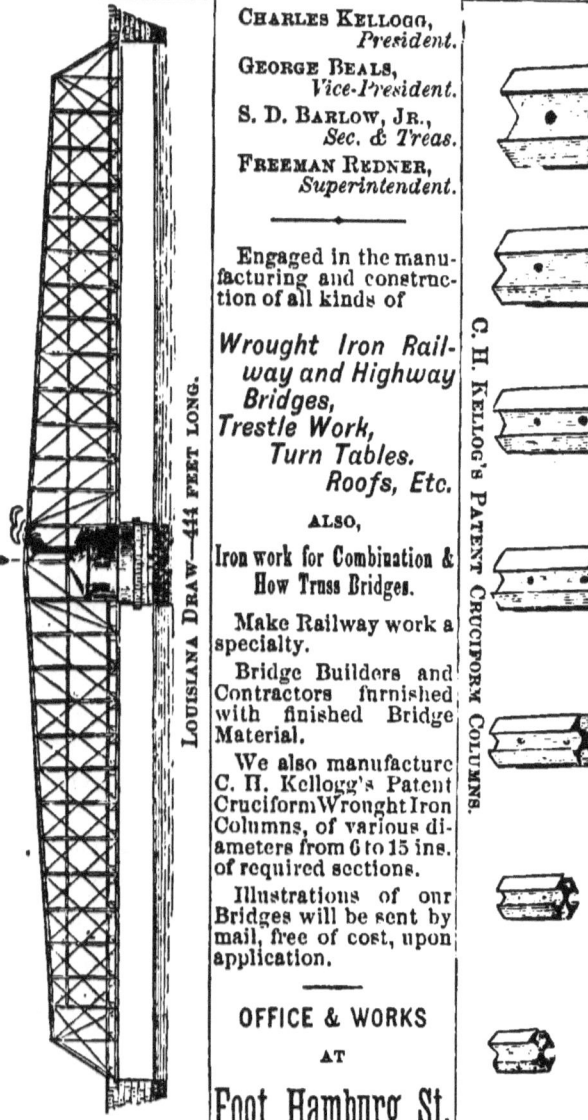

CHARLES KELLOGG, *President.*
GEORGE BEALS, *Vice-President.*
S. D. BARLOW, JR., *Sec. & Treas.*
FREEMAN REDNER, *Superintendent.*

Engaged in the manufacturing and construction of all kinds of

Wrought Iron Railway and Highway Bridges, Trestle Work, Turn Tables. Roofs, Etc.

ALSO,

Iron work for Combination & How Truss Bridges.

Make Railway work a specialty.

Bridge Builders and Contractors furnished with finished Bridge Material.

We also manufacture C. H. Kellogg's Patent Cruciform Wrought Iron Columns, of various diameters from 6 to 15 ins. of required sections.

Illustrations of our Bridges will be sent by mail, free of cost, upon application.

LOUISIANA DRAW—444 FEET LONG.

C. H. KELLOG'S PATENT CRUCIFORM COLUMNS.

OFFICE & WORKS
AT
Foot Hamburg St.

The first bridge that was thrown over these turbulent waters was constructed at the head of Goat Island in 1817. It was carried away by ice in the following Spring, and was succeeded by another, which was built in 1818, on the site of the present structure. It was built by the Messrs. Porter—extensive proprietors in this neighborhood—and was repaired in 1839 and again in 1849.

In the former year one of the workmen, named Chapin, fell from the bridge into the river; fortunately the current carried him to the first of the two small islets below. He was rescued from his perilous position by Mr. J. R. Robinson, who has more than once bravely rescued fellow-creatures from this dangerous river; and the island was named after him—Chapin Island.

Niagara Falls from Point View.

THE AMERICAN FALLS.

This is indeed a sight worth coming many hundred miles to see. Walking through the Grove, we emerge upon the Point in front of an establishment at which thousands of visitors are photographed annually in connection with the Falls. Here, at one wide sweep, we behold Niagara stretching from the American to the Canadian side in magnificent perspective. Just at our feet the smooth deep masses of the American Falls undulate convulsively as they hurl over the precipice, and dash, in a neverending succession of what we may term passionate bursts, upon the rugged rocks beneath.

Beyond, and a little to the left, is Goat Island, richly clothed with trees, its drooping end seeming as if it too were plunging, like the mighty river, into the seething abyss. Right in front of us is the great

Clarke, Holland & Co.

Having rebuilt and extensively enlarged the property formerly known as "THE EATON PLANING MILL," and having introduced a variety of new and improved wood-working machines, are prepared to offer *unsurpassed facilities* for the prompt execution of *first-class work* in every department of their business.

Doors, Sash, Blinds & Shutters

AT WHOLESALE OR RETAIL.

Particular attention paid to the manufacture of

FINE HARD-WOOD DOORS & INSIDE SHUTTERS.

Mouldings and every description of *interior finish* for building purposes, manufactured to order in hard or soft wood.

Cornices, Brackets, Verandas, Bay Windows, Stairs, &c., furnished to order.

Dressed Lumber, Flooring, Ceiling, Siding, &c., on hand or worked to order.

Machine Work carefully and promptly executed by experienced workmen.

To facilitate our business, we have now in process of erection, *four* of the celebrated

CHICAGO DRY KILNS,

with capacity for drying 40 to 50 thousand feet of lumber per day. In these, when completed, all our lumber, of every description will be *thoroughly kiln-dried before using.*

ESTIMATES furnished on application, for building material of every description.

Corner Court and Wilkeson Sts.

BUFFALO, N. Y.

Horse-Shoe Fall, uttering its deep, deafening roar of endless melody, as it plunges majestically into that curdling sea, from which the white cloud of mist rises high in air and partially conceals the background of Canada from view. This point was the last residence of Francis Abbot, the young Hermit of Niagara.

The American Fall, on the brink of which we stand, is 164 feet in perpendicular height, and 660 feet wide from the mainland to *Luna Island*. The smaller Fall, between Luna and Goat Island, is 100 feet wide. Within a short distance of the spot where we stand is the

Ferry-House.

Here there is a curious inclined plane, down which we descend in cars, which are worked by means of a water wheel and a rope; there is also a stair connected with this, at the foot of which the ferry-boat waits to convey us over to the Canadian side, whither we intend to proceed, because one of the finest views of Niagara is had from *Table Rock*. Ten minutes will be sufficient to convey us over, and the passage is quite safe. The charge is 25 cents; but before going let us hasten to the foot of the *American falls*, and view them *from below*.

Seating ourselves in the ferry-boat, we are soon dancing on the agitated waters, and gazing in profound silence and admiration at the Falls, which from this point of view are seen to great advantage. A few minutes, and we are standing on the soil of Canada. Here carriages are ready to convey us to Table Rock, little more than a mile distant. Clifton House, not far from the landing, and several other objects of interest claim our attention; but we are too full of the Great Cataract just now to turn aside, and as we shall pass this way again in descending the river, we will hasten on to behold the sublime view of Niagara from Table Rock.

Table Rock.

Table Rock is no longer the extensive platform that it once was, large portions of it having fallen from time to time. It overhangs the terrible caldron close to the Horse-Shoe Fall, and the view from it, as already described, is most sublime. In 1818, a mass of 160 feet long and 40 feet wide broke off and fell into the boiling flood; and in 1828 three immense masses fell with a shock like an earthquake. Again, in 1829, another fragment fell, and in 1850 a portion of about 200 feet in length and 100 feet thick. On one of those occasions, some forty or fifty persons had been standing on the rock a few minutes before it fell! The work of demolition still goes on, for another portion of Table Rock fell in 1857. In 1867, a large crack or seam having formed around it near the road, it was deemed unsafe, and the Canadian Government caused it to be blasted away, and now all that remains of the once famous Table Rock is a huge mass of rock at the edge of the river below the bank.

The Horse-Shoe Fall.

The view here is grand in an awful degree. An indescribable feel-

JEWETT & ROOT NEW PORTABLE RANGE.

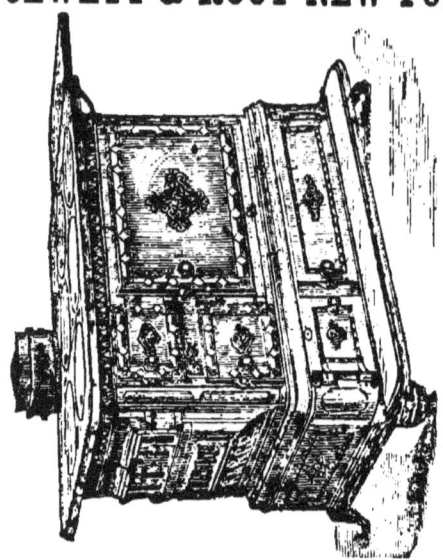

THE BEST IN MARKET.

For Sale only by

W. WOLTGE,

Housekeepers' Emporium,

No. 319 Main St.,

BUFFALO, N. Y.

Also everything useful about the Kitchen or Parlor and Dining-room.

EAGLE FILE WORKS.
CHARLES BAILEY,
FILE MANUFACTURER,

Nos. 274, 276 & 278 Court St., Buffalo, N. Y.

Old Files and Rasps re-cut, and warranted equal to new for use. Received the First Premium at the N. Y. State Fair in 1868, and at the International Industrial Exhibition, at Buffalo, in 1869.

T. TOWERS,
WHOLESALE AND RETAIL DEALER IN

BOOTS, SHOES AND RUBBERS,

ONE PRICE, LARGE SALES AND SMALL PROFITS,

No. 394 Main Street, Buffalo.

BRANCH STORE: 138 ONTARIO STREET, CLEVELAND.

Established 1869.

ing of awe steals over us, and we are more than ever impressed with the tremendous magnificence of Niagara, as we gaze upwards at the frowning cliff that seems tottering to its fall, and pass under the thick curtain of water—so near that it seems as if we could touch it—and hear the hissing spray, and are stunned by the deafening roar that issues from the misty vortex at our feet. The precipice of the Horse-Shoe Falls rises perpendicularly to a height of 90 feet; at our feet the cliff descends about 70 feet into a turmoil of bursting foam; in front is the liquid curtain which though ever passing onward, never unveils this wildest of Nature's caverns.

An enormous volume of water falls over the Horse-Shoe Fall. It is estimated that the sheet is fully 20 feet thick in the centre, an estimate which was corroborated in a singular manner in 1829. A ship named the *Detroit*, having been condemned, was bought and sent over the Falls. On board were put a live bear, a deer, a buffalo, and several smaller animals. The vessel was almost knocked to pieces in the rapids, but a large portion of her hull went over entire. She drew 18 feet water, but did not strike the cliff as she took the awful plunge.

Prospect House

stands in the rear of Table Rock. The view from the summit of this building is magnificent.

A few hundred yards above Prospect House there is a point from which we obtain a fine view of the rapids and the islands named

The Three Sisters.

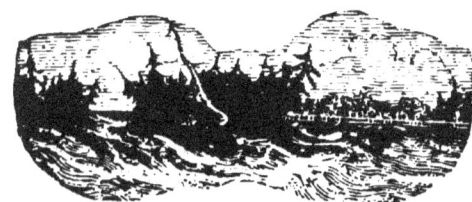

These beautiful little islands lay close together at the head of Goat Island, and are now connected by substantial foot bridges, from which the grandest views of the rapids is to be obtained.

In the Summer of 1841, before any communication was established with these islands, a gentleman named Allen was rescued from one of them by the gallant Mr. J. R. Robinson. Mr. Allen had started alone in his boat for the village of Chippewa, and in the middle of the river broke one of his oars. Being unable to gain the shore, he endeavored with the remaining oar to steer for the head of Goat Island, but the rapid current swept him past this point. As he approached the outer island of the Three Sisters, he steered with the cool energy of despair toward it and leaped ashore, while his boat sprang like a lightning flash down the rapids and over the Horse-Shoe Fall. For two days Mr. Allen remained on the island, and then, fortunately, succeeded in making a fire with some matches he happened to have in his pocket. Crowds of people assembled to assist in and witness the rescue, which was accomplished by Robinson, who, having managed to pass a rope from island to island, reached him with a skiff.

In the year 1850 another narrow escape was made here by a father and son. The son, a boy of ten years of age, was paddling his father—who was drunk at the time—over to their home on Grand Island. The father was unable to guide the frail canoe, which was carried into the rapids, and descended with fearful rapidity towards the Falls. The wretched father could do nothing to save himself; but the gallant boy struggled with the energy of a hero, and succeeded in forcing the canoe

DeWITT C. WEED & CO.

284 Main St., cor. Swan,

BUFFALO, N. Y.

DEALERS IN

BUILDERS' HARDWARE,

Cutlery, Locks, Shovels,

AGRICULTURAL IMPLEMENTS, &c.

between Goat Island and the Three Sisters. Here they were in imminent danger of passing over the little cascade between these Islands, but, providentially, as they neared it a wave upset the canoe and left them struggling in the water. The place was shallow, the boy gained a footing, and seizing his father by the collar, dragged him to the shore, where hundreds of anxious spectators received them with shouts of joy.

Gull Island is a small island just above the Horse-Shoe Fall. It has never been trodden by man.

About two miles higher up the river is

The Burning Spring.

This curious spring is very interesting. The water, being charged with sulphuretted hydrogen gas, takes fire when a light is applied to it, and burns with a pale bluish flame.

The Battle of Chippewa was fought in this neighborhood on the 5th July, 1814.

Having seen Niagara from the most striking points of view, we will now recross the river and visit Goat Island and its neighborhood.

Before crossing, let us call the attention of the reader to the celebrated

Clifton House,

which is unsurpassed for beauty of location, and healthfulness of surroundings. Being nearer the Falls than any other hotel, and the only hotel from the parlors and balconies of which a full and uninterrupted view of the rapids and Falls may be obtained, the Clifton is the most convenient and desirable resort for tourists at Niagara. Connected with the Clifton are cottages built expressly to accommodate families who prefer the quiet of a home. Terms, $3.50 per day, American currency. For families who desire to remain by the month or season, special arrangements will be made and liberal inducements offered. Messrs. Colburn & McOmber are the proprietors of this fine hotel.

Bath Island.

In a store here may be purchased any amount of Indian curiosities. The largest paper-mill in the United States is on this island. A little higher up are two smaller islets named *Ship* and *Brig* Islands. Looking down the river, we see several small islets.

Crossing the bridge at the other end of Bath Island, we reach

Goat or Iris Island.

OLD BRIDGE OVER RAPIDS.

This island is half a mile long, by a quarter broad, and contains about 70 acres. It divides the Falls, is 330 yards wide, and is heavily wooded. In 1770 a man of the name of Stedman placed some goats here to pasture; hence the name. Its other name, Iris, is derived from the number of beautiful rainbows that are so frequently seen near it. It is the property of the Porter family, and to them the public are indebted for the facilities which are afforded them in visiting the Falls. Goat Island was visited long before the

Lake Shore & Michigan Southern Railway,

Connecting with all trains from the EAST via

NEW YORK CENTRAL & HUDSON RIVER R. R.

AND ERIE RAILWAY.

THE ONLY RAILWAY Connecting with EASTERN LINES which runs all classes of Cars **THROUGH TO CHICAGO.**

Affording EQUAL ADVANTAGES to all Passengers.

Avoiding Changes and Transfers.

THROUGH TICKETS

For all Principal Points West and South-West

Can be procured at all Principal Railway Ticket Offices throughout the East, and of the Agents of this Line.

J. A. BURCH,   **CHAS. PAINE,**
Gen'l Eastern Pass'r Ag't, Buffalo.   Gen'l Sup't, Cleveland.

Toledo, Wabash & Western R'y

In connection with Eastern Lines forms the

Leading Thoroughfare via Toledo, Ft. Wayne or Danville to

St. Louis, Kansas City, St. Joseph, Atchison, Denver, Sacramento, and San Francisco.

Connecting closely at

St. LOUIS, HANNIBAL, QUINCY & KEOKUK,

For all points in

Missouri, Kansas, Texas, Colorado and California.

Pullman's Palace Sleeping Cars from Cleveland or Toledo to St. Louis or Quincy without change.

W. L. MALCOLM,
Gen'l Pass'r Agent.

bridges were constructed, but the visitors were not numerous, the risk being very great. The dates 1771, 1772, 1779, under the names of several strangers, were found cut in a beech tree near the Horse-Shoe Fall.

Three paths diverge from the house on your left, in which Indian curiosities are sold; the one to the left leads to the head of the island; the centre road cuts right across it; and that on the right conducts to the Falls. Let us follow the last mentioned through the trees that line the margin of the rapids. In a few minutes we reach a spot named *Hog's Back*, from which we have a good view of the Central and American Falls and the river below, rushing on as if in exultation after its terrific leap. Dr. Hungerford, of West Troy, was killed just under this point, in 1839, by the falling of a portion of the cliff.

That small island to our right, on the verge of the Falls, is

Luna Island,

so called because it is the best point from which to view the beautiful *lunar bow*. A narrow bridge connects this island with Goat Island.

The *lunar bow* is only seen for a short time in the month, when the moon is full and sufficiently high in the heavens.

The *solar bow* is always visible when the sun shines on the Falls.

A very melancholy accident occurred at the northern extremity of this island in the year 1849. The family of Mr. Deforest of Buffalo visited the Falls on the 21st June of that year, along with a young man named Charles Addington. They were about to leave this island when Mr. Addington playfully seized Annette, the little daughter of Mr. Deforest, in his arms, and held her over the edge of the bank, exclaiming, "I am going to throw you in." A sudden impulse of fear caused the child to bound from his grasp and fall into the rushing stream. With a loud cry of horror the young man sprang in to save her, and ere the stricken parents could utter a cry, they both went over the Falls! The next day the mangled remains of the child were discovered in the Cave of the Winds, but Addington's body was not found for several days afterwards.

The Centre Fall,

over which we pass in our return to Goat Island, although a mere ribbon of white water when seen from a short distance in contrast with the Great Falls, is by no means unworthy of notice. It is 100 feet wide, and is a very graceful sheet of water. Proceeding along the road a short distance, we come to

Biddle's Stairs.

These were erected in 1829 by Mr. Biddle, president of the United States Bank, for the purpose of enabling visitors to descend the perpendicular precipice. The stairs are firmly secured to the cliff, and are said to be quite safe. They are 80 feet high. The total descent from the top of the bank to the bottom is 185 feet.

Between this point and the Centre Fall is the spot where the celebrated *Sam Patch* made his famous leaps. Sam made two leaps in 1829. A long ladder was placed at the foot of the rock and fastened with ropes in such a manner that the top projected over the water. A platform was then laid from the top of the ladder to the edge of the bank above. Hundreds of thousands of spectators crowded every point within sight of the place on both shores, eager to behold the extraordinary spectacle of a man "jumping over the Falls." Sam walked along the giddy platform, made his bow, and went down, feet first, 97 feet into the river.

Not content with this achievement, Sam Patch afterwards made a higher leap at the Genesee Falls. Again, at the same place, he made another jump, from the height of 125 feet! That was his last. The poor fellow never rose again, and his body has never been found.

It is frequently asked by visitors where the intrepid *Blondin* crossed the river on his rope. In 1859 his rope was stretched from bank to bank about one mile below the Falls. The length of rope at this place was about 1200 feet. In 1860 he removed his rope to a point about 200 feet below the Old Suspension Bridge. The width here was 900 feet. Since then other persons, Favini, Harry Leslie and Bellini, have performed similar feats.

Before descending Biddle's Stairs, let us pass on until we reach the extremity of the island, and cross the bridge to the rocks upon which Terrapin Tower stood.

The bridge leading to these rocks is usually wet with spray, so that we must be careful in crossing. In 1852 a gentleman fell from this bridge, and was carried to the edge of the Fall; fortunately he stuck between two rocks, and was rescued by two Americans, who threw lines towards him, which he fastened round his body, and was thus drawn ashore.

Let us now descend Biddle's Stairs, and taking the road to the left, go view the

Horse-Shoe Fall from below Goat Island.

This is a terrific sight. The frowning cliff seems about to fall on us, and we are stunned by the roar of the water as it falls headlong on the broken rocks, bursts into white foam, and re-ascends in clouds of spray. Portions of the rock fall here occasionally, so that the passage is not unattended with danger.

Returning to the foot of the stairs, we follow the road to the right until we reach the famous

Cave of the Winds.

It is situated at the foot of the rock between Goat and Luna Islands, and is considered by some to be one of the finest and most wonderful sights on the American side. Here it is necessary to put on waterproof dresses and obtain a guide—both of which are at all times at our command. The cave has been formed by the action of the water on the soft substratum of the precipice, which has been washed away and the limestone rock left arching overhead 30 feet beyond the base. In front the transparent Falls form a beautiful curtain. In consequence of the tremendous pressure on the atmosphere, this cave is filled with perpetual storms, and the war of conflicting elements is quite chaotic. A beautiful *rainbow*, quite circular in form, quivers amid the driving spray when the sun shines. The cave is 100 feet wide, 130 feet high, and upwards of 30 feet deep. Along the floor of this remarkable cavern the spray is hurled with considerable violence, so that it strikes the walls and curls upwards along the roof, thus causing the rough turmoil which has procured for this place its title of the Cave of the Winds. It is much visited by ladies as well as gentlemen, and a neat building has been erected on the top of the high bank at the approach to the Biddle Stairs, which is divided into dressing rooms for persons visiting the cave.

Head of Goat Island.

The road runs quite round it. Turning to the right, in the direction of Terrapin Bridge, we observe that the rock is wearing away fast here. In 1843 an enormous mass fell from the precipice with a tremendous crash, and the rock lies near the foot of the stairs.

Passing on along the edge of the rapids, we come to the *Three Sisters* (already described); and here, between *Moss Island* and the shore, is a small but beautiful Fall, named the *Hermit's Cascade*.

From the head of Goat Island the view is very fine, the wild river and its environs being seen for a considerable distance. Navy Island, celebrated in the history of Border warfare; the sight of old Fort Schlosser on the American side; the town of Chippewa on the Canada shore; Grand Island, &c., are all visible from this point.

Niagara in Winter.

At this season Ice is the ruling genius of the spot. The spray which bursts from the thundering cataract encrusts every object with a coat of purest dazzling white. The trees bend gracefully under its weight, as if in silent homage to the Spirit of the Falls. Every twig is covered, every bough is laden; and those parts of the rocks and trees on which the delicate frost-work will not lie, stand out in bold contrast. At the foot of the Falls block rises on block in wild confusion, and the cold, dismal-looking water, hurries its green floods over the brink, and roars hoarsely as it rushes into the vortex of dazzling white below. The trees on Goat Island seem partially buried; the bushes around have almost disappeared; the houses seem to sink under their ponderous coverings of white; every rail is edged with it, every point and pinnacle is capped with it.

When the sun shines, all becomes radiant with glittering gems; and the mind is almost overwhelmed with the combined effects of excessive brilliancy and excessive grandeur. But such a scene cannot be described.

During the Winter immense masses of ice descend the river from Lake Erie, and form an Ice Bridge between the Falls and New Suspension Bridge. Hundreds of foot passengers cross this bridge during the months of February and March.

Niagara by Moonlight.

It were vain to attempt a description of this magical scene. Every one knows the peculiar softness and the sweet influence of moonlight shed over a lovely scene. Let not the traveler fail to visit Goat Island when the moon shines high and clear, and view Niagara by her pale, mysterious light.

Objects of Interest in the neighborhood of the Falls.

In enumerating these we will begin at the Cataract and descend to Lake Ontario, and will then describe the river scenery above the Falls.

New Suspension Bridge.

The New Suspension Bridge over the Niagara River is located in full view of the Great Cataract, and takes rank with any similar structure in the world for the engineering skill and commercial enterprise exhibited in its construction. It is designed more especially for foot passengers and light carriages, and will be found eminently serviceable in facilitating the sight-seeing which attracts such throngs of visitors to the Falls at all seasons—but chiefly during the Summer and the two first months of Autumn. Heretofore the means of access to the Canada side from the village of Niagara Falls, in the State of New York, has been by conveyance in hacks across the Railroad Bridge two miles below, involving a long and somewhat expensive ride. The New Bridge offers a passage from the American to the opposite shore in a walk of ten minutes from the principal hotels, with an opportunity for views of the Falls and the surrounding scenery of the most wonderful and charming description.

The elements of this new and splendid work may be gathered from the following details:

The bridge is supported upon timber towers, having a quadrilateral base of 28 feet, and converging to a square of 4 feet at the top, firmly bolted and braced, and standing upon the solid rock. The American tower is 100 feet in height; the Canadian, 105. The space from centre to centre of the towers measures 1268 feet 4 inches. It is 1190 feet from one wall of the river to the other. The suspended roadway is 1240 feet in length. The distance between the anchorages is 1828 feet; and from one anchor to the other 1888 feet. This shows it to be the longest suspension bridge in the world. The elevation of the bridge at the centre above the surface of the Niagara is from 175 to 190 feet, according to the general level of the lakes; the depth of water in the channel being 250 feet.

The two cables from which the bridge is suspended have an extreme length, as already stated, of nearly 1900 feet. They are composed of wire ropes, in number seven, each rope consisting of seven strands, and embracing 133 No. 9 wires. The cables thus consist of 931 wires. The ropes weigh 54 pounds per furlong of 6 feet. The cables are securely embedded at the extremities—on the American side 18 feet below the surface in heavy masonry, and on the other side in an excavation quarried out of the solid rock. Each of the ropes is capable of sustaining a weight of 120 tons, and their united strength is equal to 1680 tons. The over-floor stays, 48 in number, also passing over the towers and fastened in the common anchorages, will sustain an additional weight of 1320 tons. The combined strength of the cables and stays is thus found to be equal to the support of a load of 3000 tons, or 6,000,000 pounds. The weight of the bridge and its appurtenances is estimated at 250 tons—less than one-twelfth of the sustaining power depending from the towers; 3000 people may be at once distributed over the bridge, without in the slightest degree affecting its supporting capability.

The roadway of this bridge is composed of two stringers or chords, 10 feet apart, upon which are laid the cross ties, or needle-beams, 5 feet apart. The chords are further strengthened by channel bars of iron running the whole length on the under side, and so attached as to form a continuous plate. In addition, a stiff railing, 5 feet high, is erected at the sides, and so bolted to the chords and floor-beams as to serve as a protection against casualties, as well as to resist any strain from the wind, or to the transit of vehicles. The flooring consists of a double course of Norway pine, each an inch and a half thick. The roadway is 10 feet in width, sufficient to admit of the transit of foot passengers without obstruction from the passage of carriages in one direction—the latter alternating from each side of the river at periods of fifteen minutes.

A very fine view of the bridge—its cables, stays, nine hundred sus-

Sidney Shepard & Co.,

68 MAIN STREET, BUFFALO, N. Y.,

PROPRIETORS OF THE

Buffalo Stamping Works,

TRADE MARK.

MANUFACTURERS OF

FRENCH WARE, STAMPED AND JAPANNED TIN-WARE, ICE-CREAM FREEZERS, STOVE BOARDS, COAL VASES, COAL HODS, TOILET WARE, TIN TOYS, GROCERS' TINWARE. Also, a large line of miscellaneous articles.

DEALERS IN

HARDWARE & METALS,

TINMEN'S TOOLS AND MACHINES,

And Supplies of all kinds.

Illustrated Catalogue sent on application.

penders and suspender rods, and lofty towers—will be afforded from points of observation below, on the American side; and above, on the Canadian. Its great length, symmetrical form, graceful curve, and obvious strength, cannot fail to strike every beholder with equal surprise and pleasure. Whilst this structure increases the facilities for the inspection and study of the great natural wonders displayed here in such grandeur and magnificence, it is of itself an object of curious interest, and adds still another to the attractions which fill the minds of all observers with admiration.

Tolls.—50 cents for two-horse carriages, including the driver; 35 cents for one-horse carriage; 25 cents for each passenger in carriage or on foot.

The Railroad Suspension Bridge

spans the river about two miles below the Falls. We may mention, in passing, that there are two caves—*Catlin's Cave* and the *Giant's Cave*, between this Bridge and the Falls, on the American side; and *Bender's Cave* on the Canada side. They are, however, hardly worthy of notice.

This Suspension Bridge is a noble and stupendous structure. It is the work of Mr. John A. Roebling of Trenton, New Jersey, and was begun in 1852. Formerly the bridge here was of much smaller dimensions. It was begun in 1849 by Mr. Charles Elliott, who first crossed it in an iron basket, slung under a single cable of iron wire. Afterwards many people crossed in this way, being let down the incline and drawn up on the opposite side by a windlass.

The present bridge is of enormous strength, and forms a communication between Canada and the States, over which the carriages of the Great Western, New York Central and Erie Railroads, and cars of every description, run without causing the slightest vibration. The cost of its construction was $500,000 (more than £100,000 sterling); and steam carriages first crossed it on the 8th March, 1855. The road for carriages is suspended 28 feet below the railway line.

The following statistics of this enormous bridge will be interesting: The height of the towers on the American side is 88 feet; those on the Canada side are 78 feet high. Length of bridge is 800 feet; width, 24 feet; heighth above the river, 250 feet. There are four enormous wire cables of about 10 inches diameter, which contains about 4000 miles of wire; and the ultimate capacity of the four cables is about 12,400 tons. The total weight of the bridge is 800 tons; and it combines, in an eminent degree, strength with elegance of structure.

Lundy's Lane Battle-Ground

is about a mile and a half from the Falls, near to Clifton House. This great battle between the Americans and the British was fought on the 25th July, 1814. The number of killed and wounded on both sides was about equal, and both parties, as a matter of course, claim the victory!

Drummondville, in the immediate vicinity, is named after General Drummond, then commander of the British forces.

Niagara City stands on either side of the Suspension Bridge, but it is not as yet much of a city.

The Whirlpool.

About three miles below the Falls the river takes an abrupt turn, and shoots with great violence against the cliff on the Canada side, forming what is called the Whirlpool. The scenery around this caldron is exceedingly wild.

A short distance further on are the *Mineral Springs*, sometimes called the Belle Vue Fountain.

The Rapids just below the Whirlpool are very fine.

Less than half a mile further down the river, on the American side, is

The Devil's Hole,

a terribly gloomy and savage chasm in the bank of the river, between one and two hundred feet deep. Over hanging this dark cavern is a perpendicular precipice, from the top of which falls a small stream named *The Bloody Run*. The stream obtained its name from the following tragical incident:

During the French war in 1763, a detachment of British soldiers (consisting of, some say one hundred, some fifty men), was forwarded with a large supply of provisions from Fort Niagara to Fort Schlosser. The Seneca Indians, then in the pay of the French, resolved to lay an ambuscade for them, and chose this dark spot for their enterprise. The savages, who were numerous, scattered themselves along the hill-sides, and lay concealed among the bushes until the British came up and had passed the precipice; then, uttering a terrific yell, they descended like a whirlwind, and, before the soldiers had time to form, poured into their confused ranks a withering volley of bullets. The little stream ran red with blood, and the whole party—soldiers, wagons, horses, and drivers—were hurled over the cliff into the yawning gulf below, and dashed to pieces on the rocks. Only two escaped to tell the tale; the one a soldier, who returned during the night to Fort Niagara; the other a Mr. Stedman, who dashed his horse through the ranks of his enemies, and escaped amid a shower of bullets.

VIEW OF THE GREAT SUSPENSION BRIDGE OVER THE RIVER BELOW NIAGARA FALLS, CONNECTING THE GREAT WESTERN RAILWAY WITH EASTERN ROADS.

CORNELL LEAD COMPANY,
BUFFALO, N. Y.

Manufacturers of

WHITE LEAD and LEAD PIPE,

Sheet and Bar Lead.

TRADE MARK.

It has been estimated by our best painters that

PURE WHITE LEAD

Will cover one-third more surface, at one-fourth less labor, than any adulterated article used as a paint.

The CORNELL LEAD COMPANY guarantees the above Lead to be

PERFECTLY PURE,

And claim it to be equal, if not superior, to any for sale in this market.

FOR SALE BY ALL DEALERS.

Brock's Monument

stands on the Queenston Heights, Canada side, just above the village of that name. This monument was raised in commemoration of the British general, Sir Isaac Brock, who fell in the sanguinary action fought on this spot on the 13th October, 1812. His remains, and those of his aide-de-camp, Colonel John M'Donald, who died of wounds received in the same battle, are buried here.

The first monument was completed in 1826, and was blown up in 1840 by a person named Lett, who was afterwards imprisoned for this dastardly act. The present handsome shaft was erected in 1853. Its height is 185 feet; the base is 40 feet square by 30 feet high; the shaft is of freestone, fluted, 75 feet high and 30 feet in circumference, surmounted by a Corinthian capital, on which stands a statue of the gallant general.

The view from this monument is most gorgeous. The eye wanders with untiring delight over the richest imaginable scene of woodland and water. Just below is the village of Queenston, and on the opposite shore is Lewiston. In the midst flows the now tranquil River Niagara—calm and majestic in its recovered serenity. In the far distance, on either side, stretches the richly-wooded landscape, speckled with villas and cottages. At the mouth of the river are the towns of *Niagara* on the Canadian side, and *Youngston* on the American. Its entrance is guarded on the latter side by *Fort Niagara*, and on the former by *Fort Massasauga*. The whole view is terminated by the magnificent sheet of Lake Ontario, which stretches away like a flood of light to the horizon.

Queenston

is a small picturesque town, and worthy of notice chiefly on account of the memorable battle that took place on the neighboring heights.

Lewiston,

just opposite Queenston, is a beautifully situated town, about seven miles from the Falls. It is a place of some importance, and stands at the head of the navigation on the river: it contains several excellent hotels and public buildings. There is a village of Tuscarora Indians three miles from here. Lewiston was destroyed by the British in 1813, and rebuilt at the termination of the war.

Niagara Town

stands on the Canada shore, opposite Youngston, on the site of Newark, which was burnt in 1813 by General M'Clure. Its prosperity has been injured somewhat by the Welland Canal. A short distance above the town are the remains of *Fort George*, which was taken by the Americans in 1813, afterward destroyed by the British, and left in ruins.

Fort Niagara, on the American side, has many historical associations, which we have not space to touch upon. The English General Prideaux fell here in the battle of 24th July, 1759, and the French garrison afterwards surrendered to Sir William Johnson.

Fort Massasauga, at the mouth of the river, opposite Fort Niagara, is a little below the town of Niagara, and is garrisoned by British soldiers.

Niagara River above the Falls.

Grand Island, on which is a little hamlet named *White Haven*, divides the river into two branches. On the site of White Haven was intended to be built a "city of refuge for the Jews"; but the aspiring and sanguine projector failed in carrying out his intention.

J. O. ROBSON & CO.
165 Main Street, Buffalo,

Would respectfully call the attention of the public to our complete stock of

Gold and Silver
WATCHES

Key and stem winding, together with a fine lot of

Clocks, Plated Ware, Pocket Cutlery, &c.,

Double and Single Breech Loading Guns, Powder, Shot, Caps, Fishing Tackle, &c.,

All of which we offer at the lowest market prices.

J. O. ROBSON.   L. L. PIERCE.

LOST!

Forty Thousand Dollars lost in the City of Buffalo within six years. Sunk! Lost to the owners of fine buildings, manufactories, warehouses, etc., and all because of carelessness, or to save themselves twenty minutes time. Talk is cheap, but facts, "*Facts* are stubborn things," and it is a *fact* that after twenty-three years' trial it has been

FOUND

that the "Warren Roof" is without *doubt* the best roof in Buffalo. Talk may say, "Oh, they don't put on such a roof as they did twenty years ago," but if the fact of our having the *same men* to distil the material, the *same men* to put it on, the roofs from five to twenty-three years old to point to, will not convince you we will refer you to *one hundred* of the best business men of Buffalo and vicinity for information, which we think will convince the most skeptical that the *genuine* Warren Roof has great advantages over all other roofing. Space will not admit of detailing all its advantages over other roofing, but we would be glad to answer all questions and show hundreds of testimonials at the office of GUITEAU & HODGE (successors to Warren & Co.), manufacturers of and wholesale dealers in Roofing Materials, Paving Pitch, Lamp Black, Sheathing Felt, Black Varnish, Elastic Paint, Naphtha, Dead Oil, etc., etc., 283 Main street, corner Swan, Buffalo, N. Y.

Fort Schlosser, is 9 miles further down the river, on the American side. It was at the old landing here that the *burning of the Caroline* took place, during the Canadian rebellion of 1837. The insurgents had taken up a position on *Navy Island*, and the *Caroline* steamer was charged by the British with carrying provisions to the rebels. The vessel was therefore seized by Colonel M'Nabb, cut loose from her moorings, set on fire, and sent, like a flaming meteor, down the wild rapids and over the Falls of Niagara. There was no one on board when this vessel took her awful leap into the roaring gulf. Opposite Schlosser is the village of *Chippewa* (2½ miles above the Falls), from which a railway runs to Queenston and the mouth of the river. Steamers ply between Buffalo and this village, below which vessels dare not venture.

The Islands.

above the rapids are very numerous. Indeed the river is studded with them, from Lake Erie all the way down to the Falls. There are 37 of them, if we may be permitted to count those that are little more than large rocks. *Grand Island* is the largest, being 12 miles long and 7 broad. It divides the stream into two branches. *Navy Island* is just below it. Here the French built their ships of war in 1759. This island was the resort of the rebel leaders in 1837. It has an area of 304 acres. Our space forbids further notice of these islands, which are exquisitely beautiful. Some are large, and others are small; some lie in quiet water, clearly reflected in the surrounding mirror; while others stand in the midst of the raging current, looking black in the white turmoil of surrounding foam, and seeming as if they would fain check the angry waters in their headlong rush towards the Falls.

D. B. CASTLE,
Wholesale and Retail Dealer in
Gold and Silver Watches,
SILVER WARE, FANCY GOODS, &c.,
No. 161 Main Street,
Opposite the Liberty Pole, **BUFFALO, N. Y.**

Watch Repairing done in the best manner and warranted.

ORIENTAL POWDER MILLS,
MANUFACTURERS OF
GUNPOWDER,
For Sporting, Government, Shipping and Blasting.

Refined Nitre and Meal Powder for Fireworks.

A. B. YOUNG, Agent,
42 Exchange Street, - - - - - - BUFFALO, N. Y.

BIDWELL'S
Livery & Boarding Stable

409, 411 and 413 Niagara St., near Maryland.

Elegant Coaches for Parties, Funerals, &c.,

Any required number furnished on the Shortest notice.

Passengers taken to and from Cars at any Hour Night or Day.

Through Time Tables of Railroads and their Connections to be seen at our Office.

GENERAL INFORMATION.

THE CANADA SOUTHERN RAILWAY.

This road is first-class in every respect, being provided with splendid equipments in the line of Palace Parlor Cars, luxurious Sleeping Coaches, etc. It furnishes a new and desirable route to Niagara Falls by the Canada side. Trains leave the *Erie Street* depot several times daily, and pass over the new *International Bridge*, leaving passengers near the *Clifton House* and continuing on to Niagara, on the shore of Lake Ontario, where steamers leave twice daily for Toronto. This road makes connections at the Junction for Detroit and Toledo.

This is destined to become a very popular route, as the Niagara River can be seen in all its glory, and the views of the Falls from the Canada side are unsurpassed for grandeur and magnificence.

THE FINEST YET.

One of the finest trips on this continent, if not in the world, is that planned by the Erie Railway, taking you from New York to Niagara Falls, and thence via Lake Ontario and the river St. Lawrence, (passing the Thousand Islands and Rapids by daylight), to Montreal and Quebec. Returning from either of these cities to New York, your route is via Lake Memphremagog, the White Mountains, Portland, Boston, Newport, and steamers on Long Island Sound, or via Lake Champlain, Lake George, Saratoga, and day or night line steamers on Hudson river, as may be preferred. The cost of a through ticket varies from thirty to sixty dollars, depending upon the route selected.

A BEAUTIFUL ROUTE.

There seems to be a dearth of information as to the best routes of travel in this or that direction, to this or that resort. For Niagara Falls, *the Erie Railway is the route;* also for Cooperstown and adjacent watering places, including Sharon Springs. The road penetrates one of the finest and most picturesque tracts in America—the scenery varying from quiet landscape with agricultural tone, to the wildest and most Switzerland-like in the State. What with drawing-room cars, elegant sleeping cars, and other first-class appointments, the Erie, in many respects, is surpassed by no other road in the country, and under its present management promises to be successful as it has never been before.

DOMESTIC AND FOREIGN POSTAGE RATES.

LETTERS to any part of the United States, 3 cents per half ounce.
Post cards, 1 cent.

DROP OR LOCAL LETTERS at Post Office having letter carriers, 2 cents per half ounce or fraction thereof; at offices not having letter carriers the rate is 1 cent per half ounce or fraction.

NEWSPAPERS to any part of the United States, to regular subscribers, payable quarterly in advance, *weekly*, not over 4 oz., 5 cents a quarter, and 5 cents for each additional 4 oz., and an additional 5 cents for each additional issue; *dailies* six times a week being 30 cents a quarter. *All other regular periodicals sent to subscribers*, 1 cent for less than 4 ounces. Weekly newspapers free in the county where issued. *Transient Papers*, for each 2 ounces, prepaid, 1 cent each.

BOOKS, not exceeding 4 pounds in weight, 2 cents for each 2 ounces, prepaid.

CIRCULARS, unsealed, 1 cent for each two ounces prepaid, for *local* delivery, by carrier in city where mailed, 1 cent each.

SAMPLES of Merchandise, Metals, Ores, Minerals, &c., not exceeding 12 ounces in weight, 2 cents for each 2 ounces, prepaid.

MISCELLANEOUS PACKAGES, not over 2 ounces, 1 cent; and 1 cent for each additional 2 ounces, prepaid. Limited to 32 ounces, and so wrapped that the contents may be seen. These unbound miscellaneous packages include proofs, *manuscripts for books*, cards, samples, cuttings, roots, and all similar articles allowed in the mails.

REGISTRATION FEE, on letters, 8 cents each.

FOREIGN POSTAGE.—Letters to England, Ireland and Scotland, 6 cents; to France, Belgium and Holland, 10 cents; to Bremen and Hamburgh, and to any part of Germany or Austria, by the North German Union Mails, 6 cents per half ounce.

RATES OF TRAVEL PER HOUR.

A man walks	4 miles.	A moderate wind blows.	7 miles.
A horse trots	12 "	A storm moves	36 "
A horse runs	20 "	A hurricane moves	80 "
A steamboat runs	18 "	A rifle ball moves	1,000 "
A sailing vessel runs	8 "	Sound moves	743 "
Slow rivers flow	4 "	Light moves	102,000 "
Rapid rivers flow	7 "	Electricity moves	288,000 "

LANGUAGES SPOKEN.

On the whole globe at least 90,000,000 people speak the English language; about 75,000,000 the German; 55,000,000 the Spanish, and only 45,000,000 the French language.

FOREIGN AND DOMESTIC MONEY ORDER RATES.

DOMESTIC RATES.

On Order not exceeding $10		$0 05
Over $10 and not exceeding $20		0 10
" 20 " " 30		0 15
" 30 " " 40		0 20
" 40 " " 50		0 25

RATES TO ALL PARTS OF THE GERMAN EMPIRE.

On Order not exceeding $5		$0 15
Over $5 and not exceeding $10		0 25
" 10 " " 20		0 50
" 20 " " 30		0 75
" 30 " " 40		1 00
" 40 " " 50		1 25

RATES TO GREAT BRITAIN.

On Order not exceeding $10		$0 25
Over $10 and not exceeding $20		0 50
" 20 " " 30		0 75
" 30 " " 40		1 00
" 40 " " 50		1 25

RATES TO SWITZERLAND.

Orders not exceeding $10		$0 25
Over $10 and not exceeding $20		0 50
" 20 " " 30		0 75
" 30 " " 40		1 00
" 40 " " 50		1 25

UNITED STATES Treasury or National Bank Notes only received or paid on all Money Orders. No fraction of cents can be introduced in an Order.

LOFTY STRUCTURES.

The following are the heights of the principal monuments, domes, etc., in the world: St. Antoine Column at Rome, 135 feet; Principal Tower of the Smithsonian Institute at Washington, 145; Tragan's Column at Rome, 145; Napoleon's Column at Paris, 150; Washington Monument at Baltimore, 180; the Great Obelisk at Thebes, 200; Bunker Hill Monument at Boston, 225; Column of Delhi, 262; Trinity Church Steeple at New York, 264; the new Dome of the United States Capitol, 307; Dome of St. Paul's Cathedral at London, 320; Tower of Manlius, 350; Tower of the Cathedral of Strasburg, 460; Dome of St. Peter's Cathedral at Rome, 465; Great Pyramid of Egypt, 481; National Washington Monument, 517½.

PROGRESS AND IMPORTANCE OF RAILWAYS.

The subject of railway construction in this country is one of great interest and importance. Commencing no longer ago than 1830 with 23 miles, the number of miles constructed up to January, 1872, was 60,852. During 1869, the mileage constructed was 4,999; in 1870, 6,145; and in 1871, 7,453; making in the three years a total of 18,597 miles. The largest mileage in any previous year was in 1856, when it reached 3,643. During the four years of our civil war but 3,273 miles were built. The State of Massachusetts has one mile of railway to 4.86 square miles of territory. A similar ratio would give to the States of New York and Pennsylvania 10,000 miles of line respectively, and to Illinois 11,000 miles, or more than twice its present mileage. The cost of railroads in this country will average $50,000 per mile—the total for the 60,852 miles being, in round numbers, $3,000,000,000. The cost of mileage constructed in 1871, at $30,000 per mile, was about $225,000,000, while at least $50,000,000 were expended in new works and equipments on old roads, making a total expenditure for the year of $275,000,000. The rapidity of the increase of business of the railroads of the United States, and the quantity and value of their gross tonnage traffic is still more remarkable than the rapid progress of these works. In 1851 the total earnings from passengers were, for 8,838 miles, $19,274,254, and from freights $20,192,100—an aggregate of $39,466,358. In 1861, the total earnings were $130,000,000; and in 1871, $454,969,000. The tonnage of all the railroads in 1861 is estimated at 39,000,000 net tons for 31,256 miles; while, in 1871, the net tonnage was 100,000,000 tons on 60,852 miles. The net tonnage reduced to pounds of all the railroads of the country, in 1851, equaled 464 lbs. to the head of population; in 1861, 1,912 lbs.; and in 1871, 5,000 lbs. per head. The value of this tonnage per head, in 1851, equaled $35.34; in 1861, $116.92; and in 1871, $375 per head. The increase of mileage of railways constructed from 1851 to 1861 was at the rate of about 20 per cent. per annum. From 1861 to 1871 the rate of annual increase was about 10 per cent. The increase of tonnage from '51 to '61 was 50 per cent. per annum; from '61 to '71, at the rate of 23 per cent. per annum. The increase of population from '51 to '61 was at the rate of 3.5 per cent. per annum. From '61 to '71, at the rate of 2.3—10 per cent. per annum.

The cost of transporting Indian corn and wheat over ordinary highways is about 20 cents per ton per mile. At such rate the former will bear transportation only 125 miles to market, while its value is equal to 75 cents per bushel; the latter only 250 miles, while its value is $1.50 per bushel. With such highways only, our most valuable cereals will have no commercial value outside of circles having radii of 125 miles and 250 miles respectively. Upon a railroad the transportation equals 1¼ cents per ton per mile, thus increasing the circle within which corn and wheat, at the prices named, will have a marketable value to radii of 1,600 and 3,200 miles respectively. The area of a circle having a radius of 125 miles is 49,087 square miles, while that of a circle drawn upon a radius of 1,600 miles is about 160 times greater, or 8,042,406 square miles. Such a difference, enormous as it is, only measures the value of the agencies at present employed in transportation, and the results achieved compared with the old.

MILEAGE OF RAILROADS, FROM 1842 TO 1872.

The following table shows the mileage of railroads in the several States at the various periods noted, from January 1, 1842, to January 1, 1872:

	1842.	1848.	1851.	1854.	1860.	1863.	1866.	1869.	1872.
Alabama............	46	46	183	304	628	805	805	953	1671
Arkansas...........	—	—	—	—	—	38	38	86	258
California..........	—	—	—	—	23	23	214	468	1013
Connecticut........	102	202	402	496	601	630	637	637	820
Delaware	39	39	39	39	127	127	134	165	227
Florida	—	38	21	21	290	402	416	437	466
Georgia............	271	609	643	962	1371	1420	1420	1575	2108
Illinois.............	22	22	111	759	2781	2998	3157	3440	5004
Indiana............	—	42	228	1209	2014	2175	2217	2600	3529
Iowa,..............	—	—	—	—	533	731	891	1523	3160
Kansas............	—	—	—	—	—	—	40	648	1760
Kentucky..........	28	28	78	167	534	567	567	813	1123
Louisiana.........	40	40	80	89	205	335	335	335	539
Maine	11	62	245	334	472	505	521	560	871
Maryland & D. C...	259	259	259	327	277	408	446	535	820
Massachusetts.....	373	718	1035	1105	1264	1285	1297	1425	1606
Michigan..........	138	270	342	431	737	858	941	1199	2235
Minnesota.........	—	—	—	—	—	—	213	572	1612
Mississippi........	14	60	75	96	698	862	898	898	990
Missouri...........	—	—	—	38	724	838	925	1354	2580
Nebraska..........	—	—	—	—	—	—	122	920	2143
Nevada............	—	—	—	—	—	—	—	402	593
New Hampshire...	53	175	467	644	661	661	667	667	790
New Jersey........	186	185	206	347	536	633	864	973	1265
New York.........	538	761	1361	2387	2679	2728	3002	3329	4470
North Carolina....	87	87	283	420	937	937	984	1097	1190
Ohio...............	36	274	575	1200	2812	3101	3331	3398	3740
Oregon............	—	—	—	—	—	4	19	19	159
Pennsylvania......	754	1006	1240	1404	2442	3006	3728	4398	5113
Rhode Island......	50	68	68	68	108	108	125	125	136
South Carolina....	204	204	289	652	973	973	1007	1076	1201
Tennessee.........	—	—	—	291	963	1253	1296	1436	1520
Texas	—	—	—	—	284	451	465	513	865
Vermont...........	—	—	290	506	546	562	587	605	675
Virginia...........	223	303	384	752	1301	1379	1401	1464	1490
West Virginia.....	61	97	97	241	352	361	365	365	485
Wisconsin.........	—	—	20	71	826	961	1010	1235	1725
Total miles	3535	5598	9021	15360	23789	32120	35085	42245	60852

NUMBER OF MILES FROM WASHINGTON TO VARIOUS PARTS OF THE WORLD.

Auckland, N. Zealand........8160	Honolulu, S. Islands.........4650
Belize, Central America.....1410	Jerusalem, Palestine.........5490
Berlin, Germany............3840	Kingston, C. W.............. 365
Berne, Switzerland.........3720	Lima, Peru..................3180
Bremen, Germany...........3500	Lisbon, Portugal............3180
Buenos Ayres, A. R.........4870	London, England.............3300
Calcutta, India.............8580	Mexico, Mexico..............1680
Cape of Good Hope, Africa..7380	Montreal, C. E.............. 465
Cape Horn, S. A.............6450	Nicaragua, C. America.......1740
Caraccas, Venezuela.........1830	Panama, N. Grenada.........1840
Charlottetown, P. E. I...... 835	Paris, France...............3480
Chiquisaca, Bolivia.........3670	Pekin, China................7680
Constantinople, Turkey......4870	Quebec, C. E................ 590
Dublin, Ireland.............3030	Rio de Janeiro, Brazil.......4300
Edinburgh, Scotland.........3120	Rome, Italy.................4080
Frankfort, Germany.........3700	Santiago, Chili..............4700
Frederickton, N. B........... 665	St. Domingo, St. Domingo...4300
Georgetown, B. Guiana..... 2230	St. John, Newfoundland......1230
Halifax, N. S................ 750	St. Juan, Porto Rico........4380
Hamburg, Germany.........3570	St. Salvador, C. America....1650
Havana, Cuba...............1790	St. Petersburg, Russia......4290

NUMBER OF DAYS FROM ANY IN ONE MONTH TO THE SAME IN ANY OTHER.

Month.	Jan.	Feb.	Mar.	Apr.	May	J'ne	July	Aug	Sept	Oct.	Nov.	Dec.
January..........	365	31	59	90	120	151	181	212	243	273	304	334
February.........	334	365	28	59	89	120	150	181	212	242	273	303
March............	306	337	365	31	61	92	122	153	184	214	245	275
April.............	275	306	334	365	30	61	91	122	153	183	214	244
May..............	245	276	304	335	365	31	61	92	123	153	184	214
June.............	214	245	273	304	334	365	30	61	92	122	153	183
July	184	215	243	274	304	335	365	31	62	92	123	153
August...........	153	184	212	243	273	304	334	365	31	61	92	122
September.......	122	153	181	212	242	273	303	334	365	30	61	91
October..........	92	123	151	182	212	243	273	304	335	365	31	61
November	61	92	120	151	181	212	242	273	304	334	365	30
December........	31	62	90	121	151	182	212	243	274	304	335	365

EXAMPLE.—To find the number of days from the 10th May to the 10th October following. Find May in the first column, and then in a line with that under October, is 153 days. If from the 10th May to the 25th October it would be 15 days more, or 168 days; but if from the 10th May to the 1st October, it would be 10 days less, or 143 days. In leap-year, when the last day of February is included, there will be one day more.

ELECTORAL AND POPULAR VOTES FOR PRESIDENTS OF THE UNITED STATES, 1788—1872.

[*Votes as given in The New York Tribune Almanac.*]

Year of Election.	CANDIDATES.	Popular Vote.	Electoral Vote.	Whole No. of Electors.	No. of States Voting.
1788	George Washington,		69		
	John Adams,...		34	69	10
1792	George Washington, *Federal*,		132		
	John Adams,		77	132	15
1796	John Adams, *Fed.*,		71		
	Thomas Jefferson, *Republican*,		68	139	16
1800	Thomas Jefferson,* *Rep.*,		73		
	Aaron Burr, *Fed.*,		73	146	16
1804	Thomas Jefferson, *Rep.*,		162		
	Charles C. Pinckney, *Fed.*,		14	176	17
1808	James Madison, *Rep.*,		122		
	Charles C. Pinckney, *Fed.*,		47		
	George Clinton, *Democrat*,		6	175	17
1812	James Madison, *Dem.*,		128		
	De Witt Clinton, *Dem.*,		89	217	18
1816	James Monroe, *Dem.*,		183		
	Rufus King, *Fed.*,		34	217	19
1820	James Monroe, *Dem.*,		231		
	John Quincy Adams, *Dem.*,		1	232	24
1820	John Quincy Adams,* *Coalition*,	105,321	84		
	Andrew Jackson, *Dem.*,	155,872	99		
	William H. Crawford, *Dem.*,	44,282	41		
	Henry Clay, *Dem.*,	46,587	37	261	24
1828	Andrew Jackson, *Dem.*,	647,231	178		
	John Quincy Adams, *National Rep.*,	509,097	83	261	24
1832	Andrew Jackson, *Dem.*,	687,502	219		
	Henry Clay, *National Rep.*,	530,189	49		
	John Floyd,		11		
	William Wirt, *Anti-Masonic*,		7	288	24
1836	Martin Van Buren, *Dem.*,	761,549	170		
	William H. Harrison, *Whig*,		73		
	Hugh L. White,	736,656	26		
	Daniel Webster, *Whig*,		14		
	W. P. Mangum, *Whig*,		11	294	26
1840	William H. Harrison, *Whig*,	1,275,011	234		
	Martin Van Buren, *Dem.*,	1,128,702	60		
	James G. Birney, *Abolitionist*,	7,059		294	26
1844	James K. Polk, *Dem.*,	1,337,243	170		
	Henry Clay, *Whig*,	1,299,062	105		
	James G. Birney, *Abolit.*,	62,300		272	26
1848	Zachary Taylor, *Whig*,	1,360,099	163		
	Lewis Cass, *Dem.*,	1,220,544	127		
	Martin Van Buren, *Free Soil*,	291,263		290	30

* The President was elected by the House of Representatives.

PRESIDENTIAL VOTES, 1788-1872.

Year of Election.	CANDIDATES.	Popular Vote.	Electoral Vote.	Whole No. of Electors.	No. of States Voting
1852	Franklin Pierce, *Dem.*,...............	1,601,474	254	....	....
	Winfield Scott, *Whig*,...............	1,386,578	42	....	....
	John P. Hale, *Free Soil*, ...	155,825	....	296	31
1856	James Buchanan, *Dem.*,............	1,838,169	174	....	....
	John C. Fremont, *Republican*, ...	1,341,264	114	....	....
	Millard Fillmore, *American*,........	874,534	8	291	31
1860	Abraham Lincoln, *Rep.*,............	1,866,352	180	....	....
	John C. Breckinridge, *Dem.*,........	845,763	72	....	....
	Stephen A. Douglas, *Ind. Dem.*,.....	1,375,157	12	....	....
	John Bell, *Constitutional Union*,.....	589,581	39	303	33
1864	Abraham Lincoln, *Rep.*,............	2,216,067	213	....	....
	George B. McClellan, *Dem.*,........	1,808,725	21	234	26†
1868	Ulysses S. Grant, *Rep.*,............	3,015,071	214	....	....
	Horatio Seymour, *Dem.*,............	2,709,613	80	294	34‡
1872	Ulysses S. Grant, *Rep.*,............	3,597,070	300	....	....
	Horace Greeley, *Dem.* and *Lib. Rep.*,	2,834,079	....	....	....
	Charles O'Conor, *Straight Dem.*,....	....	....	....	....
	James R. Black, *Temperance*,......	....	....	....	....
	Thomas A. Hendricks,...............	....	42	....	...?
	B. Gratz Brown, *Dem.*,.............	....	18	....	....
	Charles J. Jenkins, *Dem.*,..........	....	2	....	....
	David Davis, *Dem.*..................	... .	1	366	35

† Ten States did not vote.   ‡ Three States did not vote.

The electoral votes of Louisiana 7, of Arkansas 5, and 3 of Georgia, cast for Horace Greeley, who was dead before the meeting of the Electoral College, were rejected.

Previous to the election of 1804, each elector voted for two candidates for President, and the person receiving the highest number of votes, if a majority of the whole number of electors, was declared to be President; and the person having the next highest number was Vice-President. At the first election there were 69 electors, all of whom voted for Washington, and 34 for John Adams, 35 votes being scattered upon John Jay, R. H. Harrison, J. Rutledge, Geo. Clinton, and others. At this election three States did not vote, viz: New York (8) had not passed an Electoral law; Rhode Island (3); and North Carolina (7) had not adopted the Constitution. In 1800, there was a tie vote between Thomas Jefferson and Aaron Burr, and the House of Representatives elected Jefferson on the 36th ballot, by 10 States, viz: New York, New Jersey, Pennsylvania, Maryland, Virginia, North Carolina, Georgia, Tennessee, Kentucky, and Vermont. Mr. Burr was, of course, elected Vice-President. In 1816, there was no regular Federal opposition to D. D. Tompkins for Vice-President.

MOTTOES OF THE SEVERAL STATES.

Maine.—" Dirigo." I direct, or guide.
New Hampshire.—No motto.
Vermont.—" Freedom and Unity."
Massachusetts.—" Ense petit placidam sub libertate quietem." With the sword she seeks quiet peace under liberty.
Rhode Island.—" Hope."
Connecticut.—" Qui transtulit sustinet." He who transplanted, still sustains.
New York.—" Excelsior." Higher.
New Jersey.—No motto.
Pennsylvania.—" Virtue, Liberty, and Independence."
Delaware.—" Liberty and Independence."
Maryland.—" Crescite et multiplicamini." Grow (or increase) and multiply.
Virginia.—" Sic semper tyrannis." Ever so to tyrants.
West Virginia.—" Montani semper liberi." Mountaineers are always freemen.
North Carolina.—No motto.
South Carolina.—" Animis opibusque parati." Prepared in mind and resources; ready to give life and property.
Georgia.—" Wisdom, justice, and moderation."
Florida.—" In God is our trust."
Alabama.—No motto.
Mississippi.—No motto.
Louisiana.—" Justice, union, and confidence."
Texas.—No motto.
Arkansas.—" Regnant populi." The people rule.
Tennessee.—" Agriculture and commerce."
Kentucky.—" United we stand, divided we fall."
Ohio.—No motto.
Michigan.—" Si quæris peninsulam amœnam circumspice." If thou seekest a beautiful peninsula, behold it here.
Indiana.—No motto.
Illinois.—" State Sovereignty, National Union."
Missouri.—" Salus populi suprema est lex." The welfare of the people is the supreme law.
Iowa.—" Our liberties we prize, and our rights we will maintain."
Wisconsin.—" Forward."
Minnesota.—" L'étoile du nord." The star of the north.
Kansas.—" Ad astra per aspera." To the stars through difficulties.
California.—" Eureka." I have found it.
Oregon.—" The Union."

Nebraska.—" Popular sovereignty, progress."
Washington.—"Al-ki." By and by.
Nevada.—" Volens et potens." Willing and able.
Utah.—" September 9th, MDCCCL."
Colorado.—" Nil sine numine." Nothing without God.
Dacota.—"Liberty and Union, one and inseparable, now and forever."
New Mexico. —" MDCCCL."

POPULAR NAMES OF STATES AND CITIES.

STATES.	CITIES.
Virginia—Old Dominion.	New York—Gotham.
Massachusetts—Bay State.	Boston—Modern Athens, The Hub.
Maine—Border State.	Philadelphia—Quaker City.
Rhode Island—Little Rhody.	Baltimore—Monumental City
New York—Empire State.	Cincinnati—Queen City.
New Hampshire—Granite State.	New Orleans—Crescent City.
Vermont—Green Mountain State.	Brooklyn—City of Churches.
Connecticut — Land of Steady Habits.	Washington—City of Magnificent Distances.
Pennsylvania—Keystone State.	Chicago—Garden City.
North Carolina—Old North State.	Detroit—City of the Straits
Ohio—Buckeye State.	Cleveland—Forest City.
South Carolina—Palmetto State.	Pittsburgh—Smoky City.
Michigan—Wolverine State.	New Haven—City of Elms.
Kentucky—Corn Cracker.	Indianapolis—Railroad City.
Indiana—Hoosier State.	St. Louis—Mound City.
Illinois—Sucker State.	Keokuk—Gate City.
California—Golden State.	Louisville—Fall City.
Iowa—Hawkeye State.	Nashville—City of Rocks.
Wisconsin—Badger State.	Hannibal—Bluff City.
Florida—Peninsula State.	Milwaukee—Cream City.
Texas—Lone Star State.	Buffalo—Queen City of the Lakes.

RATES OF MORTALITY.

It is generally supposed that the rate of mortality is lower in the Old World than in the New. Statistics, however, show that in Europe the annual number of deaths is 1 in every 42 inhabitants, but in this country it is 1 in every 81. In the Gulf States the average yearly proportion of deaths is 1 to every 63; in New England, 1 to 68; in the Southern States, 1 to 70; in the Atlantic and Mississippi Valley States, 1 to 80; in the Western States, 1 to 81; in the Middle States, 1 to 88; in the Pacific States, 1 to 115; in the North-western States, 1 to 120.

POPULATION OF THE PRINCIPAL CITIES OF THE UNITED STATES.—1870.

City	Population	City	Population
Allegheny, Pa.	53,180	Lewiston, Me.	13,600
Atlanta, Ga.	21,789	Lexington, Ky.	14,801
Auburn, N. Y.	17,225	Louisville, Ky.	100,753
Augusta, Ga.	15,389	Lowell, Mass.	40,928
Baltimore, Md.	267,354	Lynn, Mass.	28,233
Bangor, Me.	18,289	Manchester, N. H.	23,536
Binghamton, N. Y.	12,692	Memphis, Tenn.	40,226
Bridgeport, Ct.	18,969	Minneapolis, Minn.	13,066
Brooklyn, N. Y.	396,099	Mobile, Ala.	32,034
Buffalo, N. Y.	117,714	New Albany, Ind.	15,396
Burlington, Iowa	14,930	Newark, N. J.	105,059
Cambridge, Mass.	39,634	Newburgh, N. Y.	17,014
Chicago, Ill.	298,977	New Orleans, La.	191,418
Charleston, S. C.	48,956	New York, N. Y.	942,292
Charlestown, Mass.	28,323	Norfolk, Va.	19,229
Cincinnati, Ohio	216,239	Omaha, Neb.	16,083
Cleveland, Ohio	92,829	Oswego, N. Y.	20,910
Covington Ky.	24,505	Philadelphia, Pa.	674,022
Davenport, Iowa	20,038	Pittsburgh, Pa.	86,076
Dayton, Ohio	30,473	Portland, Me.	31,413
Detroit, Mich.	79,577	Portsmouth, N. H.	9,211
Dubuque, Iowa	18,434	Poughkeepsie, N. Y.	20,080
East Saginaw, Mich.	11,350	Quincy, Ill.	24,052
Elizabeth, N. J.	20,832	Reading, Pa.	33,930
Elmira, N. Y.	15,863	Rochester, N. Y.	62,386
Evansville, Ind.	21,830	St. Louis, Mo.	310,864
Fall River, Mass.	26,766	Salem, Mass.	24,117
Fond du Lac, Wis.	12,764	San Francisco, Cal.	149,473
Galveston, Tex.	13,818	Savannah, Ga.	28,235
Georgetown, D. C.	11,384	Springfield, Mass.	26,703
Grand Rapids, Mich.	16,507	Syracuse, N. Y.	43,051
Hamilton, Ohio	11,081	Toledo, Ohio	31,584
Hoboken, N. J.	20,297	Troy, N. Y.	46,465
Jersey City, N. J.	82,546	Utica, N. Y.	28,804
Kansas City, Mo.	32,260	Wilmington, Del.	30,841
Lancaster, Pa.	20,233	Worcester, Mass.	41,105
Leavenworth, Kan.	17,873		

Of the 35 cities of the world having over 300,000 inhabitants, 6 are in China, 5 in the United States, 5 in Great Britain, 4 in India, 3 in France, 3 in Japan, and 1 each in Turkey, Prussia, Austria, Russia, Siam, Brazil, Spain and Egypt.

POPULATION TABLES. 99

POPULATION OF THE CAPITALS OF STATES.—1870.

Washington, D. C.	109,408	Austin, Texas	4,428
Augusta, Me.	7,815	Nashville, Tenn.	28,872
Concord, N. H.	12,241	Frankfort, Ky.	5,396
Montpelier, Vt.	3,023	Columbus, Ohio	33,754
Boston, Mass.	250,526	Indianapolis, Ind.	36,565
Providence, R. I.	68,906	Springfield, Ill.	17,365
Newport, R. I.	12,521	Lansing, Mich.	5,241
Hartford, Conn.	37,180	Madison, Wis.	9,173
New Haven, Conn.	50,840	St. Paul, Minn.	20,031
Albany, N. Y.	69,422	Des Moines, Iowa	12,035
Trenton, N. J.	22,874	Jefferson City, Mo.	4,420
Harrisburgh, Penn.	23,109	Little Rock, Ark.	12,380
Dover, Del.	1,906	Topeka, Kan.	5,790
Annapolis, Md.	5,744	Lincoln, Neb.	2,441
Richmond, Va.	51,038	Denver, Colorado.	7,000
Wheeling, West Va.	19,282	Cheyenne City, Wyoming.	1,450
Raleigh, N. C.	7,790	Boise City, Idaho.	965
Columbia, S. C.	9,289	Salt Lake City, Utah	12,854
Milledgeville, Ga.	2,705	Carson City, Nevada	3,041
Tallahassee, Fla.	2,023	Virginia City, Montana	867
Montgomery, Ala.	10,588	Salem, Oregon	1,189
Jackson, Miss.	4,234	Sacramento, Cal.	16,484
Baton Rouge, La.	6,498		

POPULATION OF THE PRINCIPAL FOREIGN CITIES.

Amsterdam, Holland	275,000	Leeds, England	250,201
Athens, Greece	48,107	Lisbon, Spain	284,000
Berlin, Prussia	800,000	Liverpool, England	493,346
Berne, Switzerland	36,000	London, England	3,251,804
Birmingham, England	342,696	Madrid, Spain	298,426
Brussels, Belgium	169,249	Manchester, England	355,665
Buenos Ayres, B. A.	180,000	Munich, Bavaria	170,688
Cairo, Egypt	350,000	Paris, France (in 1870)	1,899,462
Copenhagen, Denmark	155,143	Pekin, China	1,650,000
Constantinople, Turkey	1,075,600	Quito, Ecuador	76,000
Dublin, Ireland	270,000	Rome, Italy	204,676
Edinburgh, Scotland	273,869	Stockholm, Norway	136,016
Florence, Italy	120,000	St. Petersburg, Russia	539,122
Glasgow, Scotland	440,900	Sydney, Australia	120,000
Hamburg, Germany	307,000	Teheran, Persia	85,000
Havana, Cuba	200,000	Vienna, Austria	825,165

AGGREGATE OF CENSUS RETURNS.

The following are the aggregate returns for the year ending June 1, 1870, applied to the United States:

Acres, improved	188,806,761
Acres, woodland	158,908,121
Acres, unimproved	59,366,633
Cash value of farms	$9,261,775,121
Cash value of agricultural implements	$336,890,871
Wages paid	$310,068,473
Farm products	$2,445,602,379
Value of live stock	$1,524,271,714
Wheat, bushels	267,730,931
Indian Corn, bushels	760,963,204
Rye, bushels	17,000,000
Oats, bushels	29,761,265
Buckwheat, bushels	9,821,662
Rice, pounds	73,635,021
Tobacco, pounds	262,729,540
Cotton, bales	2,993,721
Wool, pounds	102,053,264
Potatoes, bushels	143,230,000
Sweet Potatoes, bushels	21,634,000
Wine, gallons	3,096,000
Cheese, pounds	53,492,000
Butter, pounds	514,002,460
Milk, gallons	236,500,000
Hay, tons	27,416,000
Hops, pounds	28,443,600
Sugar (cane), pounds	87,043,000
Sugar (maple), pounds	28,443,000
Molasses (cane), gallons	6,600,000
Molasses (sorghum), gallons	16,041,000

NAVAL STATISTICS.

The whole tonnage of the world consists of 56,727 sail vessels, measuring 14,563,839 tons, and 4,333 steamers, measuring 3,680 670 tons. Great Britain stands first with 19,182 sail-vessels, of 5,366,327 tons, and 2,538 steamers, of 2,382,145 tons. The United States comes next, following a long way off with 7,092 ships, of 2,272,120 tons, and 420 steamers, of 401,043 tons. Norway, strange to say, comes next in the list of sail-vessels and Italy follows in the fourth place. Germany comes next, and France still next; but in the list of steamers, France is third and Germany fourth.

RELIGIOUS DENOMINATIONS OF THE UNITED STATES.

The census shows the following returns of the denominational preferences of our people in 1850, 1860 and 1870.

DENOMINATIONS.	1850.	1860.	1870.
Regular Baptists	3,247.069	3,749.551	3,907,119
Other Baptists	60,142	294,667	363,019
Congregational	807.335	956,351	1,177.212
Episcopal	643.598	817,296	991,051
Friends	286,323	269,084	224,664
Christians	303.780	691,016	865,602
Jewish	18.371	34,412	73,265
Lutherans	539.701	757.637	977,332
Methodists	4,345,519	6,259.799	6,528,209
Moravians	114,988	20.316	25,700
Mormons	10,880	13,500	87,838
Swedenborgians	5,600	15 395	18,755
Regular Presbyterians	2,079,765	2,088,838	2,198,900
Other Presbyterians	10,189	477,111	499,344
Dutch Reformed	182,686	211.068	227,228
German Reformed	160,932	273.697	431.700
Roman Catholic	667,863	1,404,437	1,990.514
Unitarians	138,067	138,213	155,471
Universalists	215,115	235,219	210,884

Bishops of the Methodist Episcopal Church—1874.

Edmund S. Janes, New York; elected 1844. Levi Scott, Odessa, Del.; elected 1852. Matthew Simpson, Philadelphia, Penn.; elected 1852. Edward R. Ames, Baltimore, Md.; elected 1852. Thomas Bowman, St. Louis, Mo.; elected 1872. William L. Harris, Chicago, Ill.; elected 1872. Isaac W. Wiley, Boston, Mass.; elected 1872. Randolph S. Foster, Cincinnati, O.; elected 1872. Stephen M. Merrill, St. Paul, Minn.; elected 1872. Edward G. Andrews, Omaha, Neb.; elected 1872. Gilbert Haven, Atlanta, Ga.; elected 1872. Jesse T. Peck, San Francisco, Cal.; elected 1872. Thomas A. Morris, Springfield, O.; elected 1836; (retired). John Wright Roberts, Monrovia, Liberia.

METHODIST EPISCOPAL CHURCH, SOUTH.

Robert Payne, Aberdeen, Miss.; elected 1846. George F. Pierce, Ga.; elected 1854. Hubbard H. Kavanaugh, Lexington, Ky.; elected 1854. William M. Wightman, Charleston, S. C.; elected 1866. David S. Doggett, Richmond, Va.; elected 1866. Holland N. McTyeire, Nashville, Tenn.; elected 1866. Enoch M. Marvin, St. Louis, Mo.; elected 1866. John C. Keener, New Orleans, La.; elected 1870.

Bishops of the Colored Methodist Episcopal Church in America.

William Henry Miles, Tennessee. L. H. Halsey. J. B. Beebe, North Carolina. Isaac Lane, Tennessee.

Bishops of the African Methodist Episcopal Church.

Daniel A. Payne, Ohio. James A. Shorter, Ohio. Alexander W. Wayman, Baltimore. Jabez P. Campbell, Philadelphia. Thomas M. D. Ward, California. John M. Brown, District of Columbia.

Bishops of the African Methodist Episcopal Zion Church.

Joseph C. Clinton. Sampson Tolbert. John J. Moore. James W. Hood. S. E. Jones. —— Brooke.

Bishops of the Moravian Church.

Samuel Reinke, Bethlehem, Pa.; consecrated 1858. Henry A. Shultz, Nazareth, Pa.; cons. 1864. David Bigler, Lancaster, Pa.; cons. 1864. Edmund de Schweinitz, Bethlehem, Pa.; cons. 1870. A. A. Reinke, New York; cons. 1870.

Bishops of the Protestant Episcopal Church in the United States—1874.

Alabama—Richard Hooker Wilmer; consecrated 1862. Arkansas—Henry Niles Pierce (missionary); cons. 1870. California—Wm. Ingraham Kip; cons. 1853. Colorado—John Franklin Spaulding; cons. 1873. Connecticut—John Williams; cons. 1851. Delaware—Alfred Lee; cons. 1841. Florida—John Freeman Young; cons. 1867. Georgia—John Watrus Beckwith; cons. 1868. Illinois—Henry John Whitehouse; cons, 1851. Indiana—Joseph Cruickshank Talbot; cons. 1860. Iowa—Henry Washington Lee; cons. 1854. Kansas—Thomas Hubbard Vail; cons. 1864. Kentucky—Benjamin Bosworth Smith; cons. 1832. Louisiana—Joseph Pere Bell Wilmer; cons. 1866. Maine—Henry Adams Neely; cons. 1867. Maryland—William Rollinson Whittingham; cons. 1840: William Pinckney, assistant; cons. 1870. Easton, Maryland—Henry Champlin Lay; cons. 1859. Massachusetts—Benjamin H. Paddock; cons. 1873. Michigan—Samuel Allen McCoskry; cons. 1836. Minnesota—Henry Benjamin Whipple; cons. 1859. Mississippi—William Mercer Green; cons. 1850. Missouri—Charles Franklin Robertson; cons. 1868. Montana—Daniel Sylvester Tuttle (missionary); cons. 1867. Nebraska and Dakota—Robert Harper Clarkson; cons. 1865. Nevada and Arizona—Ozi Wm. Whittaker; cons. 1869. New Hampshire—Wm. Woodruff Niles; cons. 1870. New Jersey—William Henry Odenheimer; cons. 1859. New York—Horatio Potter; cons. 1854. Central New York—Frederick D. Huntington; cons. 1869.

RELIGIOUS DENOMINATIONS.

Western New York—Arthur Cleveland Coxe; cons. 1865. Albany, New York—William Croswell Doane; cons. 1869. Long Island, New York—Abram Newkirk Littlejohn; cons. 1869. Niobrara and Indian Territory—William H. Hare (missionary); cons. 1873. North Carolina—Thomas Atkinson; cons. 1853: Theodore Lyman, assistant; cons. 1872. Ohio—Gregory Thurston Bedell; cons. 1858. Oregon—Benjamin Wistar Morris (missionary): cons. 1868. Pennsylvania—William Bacon Stevens; cons. 1862. Pittsburg, Pennsylvania—John Barrett Kerfoot; cons. 1866. Central Pennsylvania—Mark Antony de Wolfe Howe; cons. 1871. Rhode Island—Thomas March Clark; cons. 1854. South Carolina—William Bell White Howe; cons. 1871. Tennessee—Charles Todd Quintard; cons. 1865. Texas—Alexander Gregg; cons. 1859. Vermont—William Henry Augustus Bissell; cons. 1868. Virginia—John Johns; cons. 1842: Francis McNeece Whittle, assistant; cons. 1868. Wisconsin—William Edmond Armitage; cons. 1866. Channing Moore Williams, China and Japan (missionary); cons. 1866. John Gotlieb Auer, Cavalla, Africa, (missionary); cons. 1873. John Payne, late of Cape Palmas, Africa, (retired); cons. 1851. Horatio Southgate, late of Constantinople, Turkey, (retired); cons. 1844.

Hierarchy of the Roman Catholic Church in the United States—1873.

ARCHBISHOPS.—James Rooseveldt Bayley, D. D., Baltimore. John Baptist Purcell, D. D., Cincinnati. Napoleon I. Perche, D. D., New Orleans. John McCloskey, D. D., New York. Francis Norbert Blanchet, D. D., Oregon. Peter Richard Kenrick, D. D., St. Louis. Joseph S. Alemany‘ D. D., O.S.D., San Francisco.

BISHOPS—PROVINCE OF BALTIMORE.—Baltimore, Md.—Archbishop Bayley. Erie, Pa.—Tobias Mullen. Philadelphia, Pa.—James F. Wood. Pittsburg, Pa.—M. Domenec. Scranton, Pa.—William O'Hara. Harrisburg, Pa.—Jeremiah W. Shanahan. Wilmington, Del.—Thomas A. Becker. Richmond, Va.—James Gibbons. Savannah, Ga.—William H. Gross, Wheeling, West Va.—Richard V. Whelan. North Carolina—Right Rev. James Gibbons, administrator. Charleston, S. C.—P. N. Lynch. St. Augustine, Fla.—Augustin Verot.

PROVINCE OF CINCINNATI.—Cincinnati, O.—Archbishop Purcell. Columbus, O.—Sylvester H. Rosecrans. Cleveland, O.—Richard Gilmour. Covington, Ky.—A. M. Toebbe. Detroit, Mich.—C. H. Borgess. Fort Wayne, Ind.—Joseph Dwenger. Louisville, Ky.—William McCloskey. Marquette, Wis.—Ignatius Mrack. Vincennes, Ind.—Maurice de St. Palais.

PROVINCE OF NEW ORLEANS.—New Orleans, La.—Archbishop Perche. Galveston, Texas—M. Dubuis. Little Rock, Ark.—Edward Fitzgerald.

Mobile, Ala.—John Quinlan. Natchez, Miss.—William Henry Elder. Natchitoches, La.—Augustus Martin.
PROVINCE OF NEW YORK.—New York, N. Y.—Archbishop McCloskey. Albany, N. Y.—John J. Conroy. Albany, N. Y.—F. McNeirney, coadjutor. Rochester, N. Y.—Bernard J. McQuaid. Boston, Mass.—P. J. O'Reilly. Brooklyn, N. Y.—John Loughlin. Buffalo, N. Y.—Stephen Vincent Ryan, C.M. Burlington, Vt.—Louis de Groesbriand. Hartford, Conn.—Francis P. McFarland. Newark, N. J.—M. A. Corrigan. Portland, Me.—David W. Bacon. Providence, R. I.—Thos. F. Hendricken. Ogdensburg, N. Y.—Edgar P. Wadhams.
PROVINCE OF OREGON.—Oregon City—Archbishop Blanchet. Nesqualey—M. A. Blanchet.
PROVINCE OF ST. LOUIS—St. Louis, Mo.—Archbishop Kenrick. St. Louis, Mo.—P. J. Ryan, coadjutor. St. Joseph, Mo.—John Hogan. Alton, Ill.—P. J. Baltes. Chicago, Ill.—Thomas J. Foley. Dubuque, Iowa—John Hennessy. Milwaukee, Wis.—John Martin Henni. Green Bay, Wis.—Joseph Melcher. La Crosse, Wis.—Michael Heiss. Nashville, Tenn.—P. A. Feehan. Santa Fé, New Mexico—John Lamy. St. Paul, Minn.—Thomas L. Grace, O.S.D. Kansas and the Indian Territory east of the Rocky Mountains—John B. Miege, Louis Fink, Leavenworth City, Kansas. Vicariate Apostolic of Nebraska—James O'Gorman. Vicariate Apostolic of Idaho — Louis Lootens. Vicariate Apostolic of Colorado and Utah—J. Projectus Machebœuf.
PROVINCE OF SAN FRANCISCO.—San Francisco—Archbishop Joseph S. Alemany, D. D., O.S.D. Monterey—Thaddeus Amat, C.M. Monterey—F. Mora, coadjutor. Grass Valley, Cal.—Eugene O'Connell.

THE NAME OF GOD IN FORTY-EIGHT LANGUAGES.

Hebrew—Elohim, or Eloah. Chaldaic—Elah. Assyrian—Ellah. Syriac, Turkish—Alah. Malay—Alla. Arabic—Allah. Language of the Magi—Orsi. Old Egyptian—Zent. Armorian—Tenti. Modern Egyptian—Tenn. Greek—Theos. Æolian, Doric—Ilos; Latin, Deus; Low Latin, Diex. Celtic, Old Gallic—Dieu. French—Dieu. Spanish —Dios. Portuguese—Deos. Old German—Diet. Provencal—Dion. Low Breton—Done. Italian—Dio. Irish—Die. Olala Tongue—Deu. German and Swiss—Gott. Flemish—Goed. Dutch—Godt. English and Old Saxon—God. Teutonic—Goth. Danish and Swedish—Gut. Norwegian—Gud. Slavic—Buch. Polish—Bog. Polacca—Bung. Lapp—Jubinal. Finnish—Jumala. Runic—As. Pannonian—Istu. Tembloan—Fetiyo. Hindostance—Rain. Caromdel—Brama. Tartar —Magatal. Persian—Sire. Chinese—Pussa. Japanese—Goergun. Madagascar—Tannan. Peruvian—Puchocamae.

COMMERCE OF THE WORLD.

FRANCE exports wines, brandies, silks, furniture, jewelry, clocks, watches, paper, perfumery, and fancy goods generally.

PRUSSIA exports linens, woolens, zinc, iron, copper and brass, indigo, wax, hams, musical instruments, tobacco, wine, and porcelain.

GERMANY exports wool, woolen goods, linens, rags, corn, timber, iron, lead, tin, flax, hemp, wine, wax, tallow, and cattle.

AUSTRIA exports minerals, silk, thread, glass, wax, tar, nut gall, wine, honey, and mathematical instruments.

ENGLAND exports cottons, woolens, glass, hardware, earthenware, cutlery, iron, metallic wares, salt, coal, watches, tin, silks, and linens.

SPAIN exports wines, brandies, iron, fresh and dried fruits, quicksilver, sulphur, salt, cork, saffron, anchovies, silks and woolens.

CHINA exports tea, rhubarb, musk, ginger, borax, zinc, silks, cassia, filigree work, ivory ware, lacquered ware, and porcelain.

BRAZIL exports coffee, indigo, sugar, rice, hides, dried meats, tallow, gold, diamonds, and other stones, gums, mahogany, and india rubber.

WEST INDIES export sugar, molasses, rum, tobacco, cigars, mahogany, dye-wood, coffee, pimento, fresh fruit and preserves, wax, ginger, and other spice.

EAST INDIES export cloves, nutmegs, mace, pepper, rice, indigo, gold dust, camphor, benzine, sulphur, ivory, rattans, zinc, and nuts.

UNITED STATES export principally agricultural produce, tobacco, cotton, flour, provisions of all kinds, lumber, and turpentine.

WEIGHTS AND MEASURES.

BUSHEL.	POUNDS.	BUSHEL.	POUNDS.
Wheat	60	Blue Grass Seed	14
Shelled Corn	56	Buckwheat	52
Corn in the Ear	70	Dried Peaches	38
Peas	60	Dried Apples	24
Rye	56	Onions	57
Oats	32	Salt	50
Barley	47	Stone Coal	80
Irish Potatoes	60	Malt	38
Sweet Potatoes	55	Bran	20
White Beans	62	Turnips	55
Castor Beans	46	Plastering Hair	9
Clover Seed	60	Unslacked Lime	50
Timothy Seed	45	Corn Meal	50
Flaxseed	56	Fine Salt	55
Hempseed	44	Ground Peas	22 and 28

WAR RECORD OF THE REBELLION.
1861.
Fort Sumter.—Captured, April 14.
Big Bethel, Va.—National repulse, June 10.
Boonville, Mo.—Confederate defeat, June 17.
Carthage, Mo.—Indecisive. July 6.
Rich Mountain, W. Va.—National victory, July 10.
Bull Run, Va.—National defeat, July 21.
Wilson's Creek, Mo.—Confederate defeat, August 10.
Hatteras Expedition.—Forts Hatteras and Clark captured, Aug. 26-30.
Carnifex Ferry, Va.—Floyd defeated by Rosecrans, September 10.
Lexington, Mo.—Taken by Confederates, September 20.
Santa Rosa Island.—Confederate defeat, October 9.
Ball's Bluff, Va.—Baker defeated and killed, October 21.
Port Royal Expedition.—Capture of Hilton Head, S. C., Oct. 29-Nov. 7.
Belmont, Mo.—Indecisive. November 7.
1862.
Middle Creek, Ky.—Garfield defeats Marshan, January 10.
Mill Spring, Ky.—Zollicoffer defeated and killed, January 19.
Fort Henry, Tenn.—Captured by Com. Foote, February 6.
Roanoke Island.—National victory, February 7-8.
Fort Donelson.—Surrendered to Grant, February 16.
Valverde, N. M.—Canby defeats Sibley, February 21.
Pea Ridge, Ark.—Confederate defeat, March 7-8.
Hampton Roads, Va.—Monitor and Virginia, March 9.
Pittsburg Landing, Tenn.—Indecisive. April 6-7.
Island No. 10.—Surrendered to Pope, with 6,000 prisoners, April 7.
New Orleans.—Captured by the Nationals, April.
Williamsburg, Va.—Confederate defeat, August 5
Winchester, Va.—Banks driven, May 25.
Hanover Court House, Va.—Confederate repulse, May 27.
Seven Pines and Fair Oaks, Va.—Confederate repulse, May 31-June 1.
Memphis, Tenn.—Captured by Nationals, June 6.
Cross Keys and Port Republic, Va.—National repulse, June 8-9.
Mechanicsville, Cold Harbor, Savage's Station, Frazier's Farm, and Malvern Hill, Va.—The seven days battles, June 26-July 1.
Baton Rouge, La.—Breckenridge defeated, August 5.
Cedar Mountain, Va.—Banks defeated, August 9.
Bull Run.—Second battle, Pope's defeat, August 30.
South Mountain, Md.—National success, September 14.
Harper's Ferry.—Surrendered, with 10,000 National prisoners, Sept. 15.
Antietam, Md.—National success, September 17.
Iuka, Miss.—Confederate defeat, September 19-20.

WAR RECORD OF THE REBELLION. 107

Corinth, Miss.—Confederate defeat, October 3.
Perryville, Ky.—Indecisive. October 8.
Prairie Grove, Ark.—Confederate defeat, December 7.
Fredericksburg, Va.—Burnside defeated by Lee, December 13.
Holly Springs, Miss.—Captured by Van Dorn, December 20.
Chickasaw Bayou, Miss.—Sherman repulsed, December 27-29.
Stone River (Murfreesborough), Tenn.—Confederate defeat, December 31, 1862–Jan. 3, 1863

1863.

Arkansas Post, Ark.—Captured by J. A. McClernand, January 11.
Raids by Grierson, in Mississippi; Stoneman, in Virginia, and Streight, in Northern Georgia, April 11–May 5.
Port Gibson, Miss.—Confederate defeat, May 1.
Chancellorsville, Va.—Indecisive. May 1-4.
Raymond, Miss.—Confederate defeat, May 12.
Jackson, Miss.—Confederate defeat, May 14.
Champion Hill, Miss.—Confederate defeat, May 16.
Big Black, Miss.—Confederate defeat, May 17.
Vicksburg.—Two unsuccessful assaults, May 19-22.
Port Hudson.—Assault repulsed, May 27.
Hanover Junction, Va.—National success, June 30.
Gettysburg, Pa.—Lee defeated by Meade, July 1-4.
Vicksburg, Miss.—Surrendered to Grant, July 4.
Helena, Ark.—Confederate defeat, July 4.
Port Hudson, La.—Surrendered to Banks, July 9.
Jackson, Miss.—Johnson driven by Sherman, July 16.
Fort Wagner, S. C.—Captured, September 6.
Morgan's Raid, Kentucky, Indiana and Ohio.—June 24–July 26.
Chickamauga, Ga.—Rosecrans defeated, but retains Chattanooga, September 19-20.
Campbell's Station, Tenn.—Longstreet checked by Burnside, Nov. 16.
Lookout Mountain, Tenn.—Stormed by Hooker's troops, Nov. 24.
Mission Ridge.—Bragg's defeat, November 25.

1864.

Olustee, Fla.—National defeat, February 20.
Sabine Cross-Roads, La.—National defeat, April 8.
Pleasant Hill, La.—Confederate repulse, April 9.
Fort Pillow, Tenn.—Capture and massacre, April 12.
Wilderness, Va.—Indecisive. May 5-6.
Resaca, Ga.—National victory, May 14-15.
Spottsylvania Court-House, Va.—Indecisive. May 7-12.
Petersburg, Va—Butler's attack, May 10.
New Hope Church, Ga.—Indecisive. May 25.

Cold Harbor, Va.—Grant repulsed, June 1-3.
Petersburg.—Smith's attack, June 16.
Weldon Railroad.—National repulse, June 21-22.
Kenesaw Mountain.—Sherman repulsed, June 27.
Peach-Tree Creek.—Indecisive. July 20.
Decatur, Ga.—Indecisive. July 22.
Atlanta, Ga.—Hood repulsed, July 28.
Petersburg, Va.—Mine explosion, National repulse, July 30.
Jonesborough, Ga.—National victory, August 31-September 1.
Atlanta, Ga.—Captured by Sherman, September 2.
Winchester, Va.—Sheridan defeats Early, September 19.
Fisher's Hill.—Sheridan defeats Early, September 22.
Alltoona Pass, Ga.—Hood repulsed, October 6.
Hatcher's Run, Va.—Grant repulsed, October 27.
Fort M'Allister, Ga.—Captured, December 14.
Nashville, Tenn.—Hood's defeat, December 15-16.

1865.

Five Forks, Va.—Lee defeated, March 31-April 1.
Averysborough, N. C.—Confederate repulse, March 16.
Bentonville, N. C.—Confederate repulse, March 18.
Fort Fisher.—Captured by Terry, January 15.
Hatcher's Run, Va.—Second National repulse, February 5.
Petersburg, Va.—Carried by assault, April 2.
Mobile.—National victory, April 8-12.

TOTAL STATISTICS OF THE LAST UNITED STATES CENSUS.

The total population of the country is about thirty-eight and a quarter millions. Total number of deaths in the current census year, 492,263, or about 1,349 per diem. March seems to be the most fatal month, leading all others by about 1,000. The births number 1,110,475, or about 3,000 per diem. The blind number about 20,000; the deaf and dumb about 16,000; the idiotic about 24,000; the insane about 37,000—nearly one-third of whom are of foreign birth. Persons over 80 years of age number about 150,000; over 90 years of age number 7,000; over 100 number 3,500. Of those over 80, females out-number males by about 12,000; of those over 90, the females are in excess by about 1,200; of those over 100, the females exceed the males by about 1,000.

On March 6th, 1786, the enormous sum of £471,000 was paid by England to the Landgrave of Hesse, for Hessian "auxiliaries" (mercenaries) lost in the American War.

USEFUL AND CURIOUS MEMORANDA.

[*Compiled by W. T. Horner from Haydn's Dictionary of Dates.*]

Ark of the Covenant.—Constructed 1492 B. C.

Babel, Tower of—Built 2247 B. C.

Babylon.—Founded by Belus, 2245 B. C.

Ball's Bluff, Battle of—On Potomac, October 21, 1861.

Bank of North America.—The first in the United States chartered by Congress, 1781, and by the State of Pennsylvania, 1782.

Battles.—Joshua subdues the five kings of Canaan, 1451 B. C.; Troy taken and destroyed, 1184 B. C.; Punic wars began, 264 B. C.; Fort Sumter captured by the Confederates, April 14th, 1861.

Cæsars.—The era of the Cæsars is reckoned from the 1st of January, 38 B. C.

Calendar.—The Roman calendar, which has in great part been adopted by almost all nations, was introduced by Romulus, 738 B. C., who divided the year into 10 months, comprising 304 days. This year was of 50 days less duration than the lunar year and of 61 less than the solar year, and its commencement did not correspond with any fixed season. Numa Pompilius, 713 B. C., corrected this calendar by adding 2 months; and Julius Cæsar, 45 B. C., desirous to make it more correct, fixed the solar year at 365 days and six hours, every fourth year being bissextile or leap-year. This almost perfect arrangement was called the Julian style and prevailed generally throughout the Christian world till the time of Pope Gregory XIII. The calendar of Julius Cæsar was defective in this particular, that the solar year consisted of 365 days, 5 hours and 49 minutes, and not of 365 days and six hours. This difference amounted to 10 entire days, the vernal equinox falling on the 11th instead of on the 21st of March. To obviate this error, Gregory ordained, in 1582, that *that* year should consist of 356 only (October 5th became October 15th): and to prevent farther irregularity, it was determined that a year beginning a century should not be bissextile, with the exception of that beginning each fourth century: thus 1700 and 1800 have not been bissextile, nor will 1900 be so; but 2000 will be a leap-year. In this manner 3 days are retrenched in 400 years, because the lapse of 11 minutes makes 3 days in about that period. The year of the calendar is thus made as nearly as possible to correspond with the true solar year, and future errors of chronology are avoided.

Chemistry.—Introduced into Europe by the Spanish Moors about 1150 A. D.

Coliseum at Rome.—Supposed to have been able to contain 80,000 spectators of the fights of wild beasts. It was erected between 75 and 80 A. D., by Emperors Vespasian and Titus.

Damascus.—A city in the time of Abraham, 1913 B. C.

Evangelical Alliance.—Founded by Sir Culling Eardley Smith and others, at Liverpool, in 1845.

February.—(From Februus, an Italian divinity.) This month, with January, was added to the year by Numa, 713 B. C.

Fire Engines are said to have been invented by Ctesibius, 250 B. C. They are mentioned by Pliny, A. D. 70.

Guillotine.—Invented about 1785 by Joseph Ignatius Guillotin, an eminent physician and senator, designed to render capital punishment less painful.

High and Low Church.—These sections in the Church of England began in the reign of Anne, 1709.

Honey-moon.—Among the ancients, a beverage prepared with honey, such as that known as mead. It was a custom to drink of diluted honey for thirty days, or a moon's age, after a wedding feast, and hence arose the term Honey-moon, of Teutonic origin.

Hymns.—The Song of Moses (Exod. xv.) is the most ancient—1491 B. C. The Psalms date from about 1060 B. C. to about 444 B. C. (from David to Ezra). Hilary, the Bishop of Arles, in France, is said to have been the first who composed hymns to be sung in Christian churches, about A. D. 431.

Ides.—In the Roman calendar the thirteenth day of each month, except in March, May, July and October, in which it was the fifteenth day.

January derives its name from Janus, an early Roman divinity. Numa made it the first month because Janus was supposed to preside over the beginning of all business. In 1751 the legal year was ordered to begin in England on January 1, instead of March 25.

Juries.—The trial by jury was introduced into England during the Saxon Heptarchy, according to *Lambards*, but by most authorities their institution is ascribed to Alfred, about 886 A. D.

Kissing the hands of great men was a Grecian custom. Kissing was a mode of salutation among the Jews. The kiss of charity, or "holy kiss," commanded in the Scriptures, was observed by the early Christians, and is still recognized by the Greek Church and some others. Kissing the Pope's foot began with Adrian I. or Leo III., at the close of the 8th century.

Koran, the sacred book of the Mohammedans, was written about 610 A. D. by Mohammed.

Lady.—The masters and mistresses of manor-houses in former times served out bread to the poor, weekly, and were, therefore, called *Lafords* and *Lefdays*, signifying bread-givers (from *hlaf*, a loaf), hence Lords and Ladies.

Labyrinth.—Four are mentioned: the first is said to have been built by Daedalus, in the Island of Crete, about 1210 B. C. The second in Egypt, in the Isle Mocris, by Psammetichus, king of that place, about 683 B. C. The third at Lemnos. The fourth at Clusium, in Italy, erected by Porsenna, King of Etruia, about 520 B. C. Labyrinths were buildings constructed with a multitude of winding passages, so that a person could hardly avoid being lost.

Leap-Year, or Bissextile, originated with astronomers of Julius Cæsar, 45 B. C. They fixed the solar year at 365 days, 6 hours, from one vernal equinox to another; the six hours were set aside, and at the end of four years forming a day, the fourth year consisted of 365 days. The day thus added was called intercalary, and was placed a day before the 24th of February, the sixth of the calends, which was reckoned twice, hence called bissextile or twice sixth. This added day with us is February 29th.

Libraries.—The first public library of which we have any account in history was founded at Athens by Pisistratus, about 544 B. C. The second of note was founded by Ptolemy Philadelphus, 284 B. C. It was partially destroyed when Julius Cæsar set fire to Alexandria, 47 B. C. 400,000 valuable books in MS. are said to have been lost by this catastrophe. According to Plutarch, the library of Pergamos contained 200,000 books. It came into the possession of the Romans at the death of Attalus III. (133 B. C.) The first private library was the property of Aristotle, 334 B. C.—*Strabo*. The first library at Rome was instituted 167 B. C.; it was brought from Macedonia.

Magna Charta.—The fundamental parts of the great charter of English liberty were derived from Saxon charters continued by Henry I. and his successors. It was signed by John at Runnymede, near Windsor, June 15, 1215.

Mausoleum.—Artemesia married her own brother, Mausolus, King of Caria, Asia Minor, 377 B. C. At his death she drank in liquor his ashes after his body had been burned, and erected to his memory at Halicarnassus a monument, one of the seven wonders of the world (350 B. C.), termed Mausoleum.

Mendicant Friars.—Several religious bodies commenced alms-begging in the 13th century, in the pontificate of Innocent III. They spread over Europe and embraced many communities, till at length by general council, held by Gregory X., at Lyons in 1272, were confined to four orders—Dominicans, Franciscans, Carmelites and Augustines. The Capuchins and others branched off.

Mint of the United States was established by act of Congress in April, 1792, but it was not put into full force until January, 1795. The act specified that the gold coin should be of the fineness of 22 carats.

Mensuration.—The various properties of conic sections were discovered by Archimedes, to whom the chief advancement in mensuration may be attributed. He also determined the ratio of spheres, spheroids, etc. (218 B. C.).

Monroe Doctrine.—A term applied to a determination expressed by James Monroe, President of the United States, 1817-21, not to permit any European power to interfere in restraining the progress of liberty in North or South America, by exercising sovereignty on this continent.

Needles were first made in England, in Cheapside, London, in the time of Mary I., by a negro from Spain, but was lost at his death, and not recovered till 1566, in the reign of Elizabeth.—*Stow.*

Oxygen.—A gas, and is the most abundant of all substances, constituting about one-third of the solid earth, and forming by weight nine-tenths of water and one-fourth of the atmosphere.

Paper is said to have been invented in China, 170 B. C. It was first made of cotton about A. D. 1000, and of rags about 1300.

Plus (+) *and Minus* (−).—Prof. De Morgan attributes these signs to either Christopher Rudolf, about 1522, or Michael Stifelius, about 1544.

Potatoes.—Natives of Chili and Peru.

Printing—With blocks, by John Koster of Haarlem, 1438. John Fust established a printing office at Mentz, 1442. John Guttemberg invented cut metal types and used them in printing the earliest edition of the Bible, which was commenced 1444 and finished in 1460. Peter Schœffer cast the first metal types in matrices, and therefore was the inventor of complete printing, 1452. Book of Psalms printed by Fust and Shœffer, August 14, 1457. Printing for the blind (by raised characters) begun in 1827.

Punctuation.—The ancients do not appear to have had any system, and doubtless employed arbitrary signs to distinguish the parts of a discourse. Of our points the period (.) is the most ancient. The colon (:) was introduced about 1485; the comma (,) was first seen about 1521; and the semi-colon (;) about 1570. In Sir Philip Sidney's "Arcadia" (1587) they all appear, as well as the note of interrogation (?), asterisk (*) and parenthesis ( ).

Rome.—The foundation of the city by Romulus was laid on the 20th of April, according to Varro, in the year 3961 of the Julian period (3251 years after the creation of the world, 753 years before the birth of Christ, 431 years after the Trojan war, and in the fourth year of the sixth Olympiad). Other dates given: Cato, 751 B. C.; Polybus, 750; Fabius Pictor, 747; Cincius, 728. In the time of Julius Cæsar the empire was bounded by the Euphrates, Taurus and Armenia on the east; by Æthiopia on the south; by the Danube on the north, and by the Atlantic on the west.

Quarantine.—The custom was first observed at Venice, 1127, whereby all merchants and others coming from the Levant were obliged to remain in the house of St. Lazarus forty days before they were admitted into the city.

Sabbath Schools.—The first Sabbath School was founded by Ludwig Hacker, between the years 1740 and 1747, at Ephrata, Pa. The school room was used as a hospital after the battle of Brandywine, fought in 1777. This event occasioned the breaking up of the school, about five years before the first Sabbath School was instituted in England by Robert Raikes, about 1782.

September.—The seventh Roman month reckoned from March. It became the ninth month when January and February were added to the year by Numa, 713 B. C.

Septuagent version of the Bible was made from the Hebrew into the Greek, 277 B. C. Seventy-two translators were shut up in thirty-six cells; each pair translated the whole, and on subsequent comparison, the thirty-six copies did not vary but a word or letter.—*Justin Martyr.*

Tabernacle—The Holy Place of the Israelites, till the erection of Solomon's Temple, 1491 B. C.

Tin.—The Phœnicians traded with England for this article for more than 1100 years before the Christian era.

Urim and Thummim.—Light and perfection. The *urim* and *thummim* were worn as ornaments or decorations in the breastplate of the high priest when he attended the altar; but what they were has never been satisfactorily ascertained.

Vulgate (from *vulgatus*, published).—A term applied to the Latin version of the Scriptures which is authorized by the Council of Trent (1546), and which is attributed to St. Jerome, about 384.

Writing.—Pictures were undoubtedly the first essay toward writing. The most ancient remains of writing which have been transmitted to us are upon hard substances, such as stones and metals used by the ancients for edicts. Athotes, or Hermes, is said to have written a history of the Egyptians, and to have been the author of the hieroglyphics, 2112 B. C.

Xerxes crossed the Hellespont by a bridge of boats, and entered Greece in the Spring of 480 B. C. with an army and retinue amounting to 5,283,220 souls.

Yard.—The precise origin of our yard is uncertain. It is, however, likely that the word is derived from the Saxon *gyrd*, a rod or shoot, or *gyrdan*, to enclose—being anciently the circumference of the body, until Henry I. decreed that it should be the length of his arm.

Zinc.—This ore was known to the Greeks, who used it in the manufacture of brass.

UNIVERSAL HISTORY.

[*Compiled by W. T. Horner, A. M., from Putnam's Dictionary of Dates.*]

I. ANCIENT HISTORY.

Period I.—The Ante-diluvian; 1656 years.

Period II.—Dispersion of mankind; 427 years. The deluge to Abraham.

Period III.—The Abrahamic or Patriarchal; 430 years. Abraham to Moses.

Period IV.—The Mosaic or Theocratic; 396 years. Moses to Saul.

Period V.—The Monarchical; 489 years. Saul to Cyrus.

Period VI.—The Persian; 322 years. Cyrus to Alexander.

Period VII.—The Grecian; 184 years. Alexander to the fall of Greece.

Period VIII.—The Roman; 146 years. Fall of Greece to the Christian era.

II. MODERN HISTORY.

Period I.—306 years. From the Christian era to the reign of Constantine.

Period II.—170 years. Constantine to Odoacer.

Period III.—146 years. Odoacer to Mahomet.

Period IV.—178 years. Mahomet to Charlemagne.

Period V.—266 years. Charlemagne to William the Conqueror.

Period VI.—233 years. William the Conqueror to Othman 1st.

Period VII.—154 years. Othman to the fall of the Eastern Empire.

Period VIII.—145 years. Fall of the Eastern Empire to the Edict of Nantes.

Period IX.—120 years. Edict of Nantes to the death of Charles XII. of Sweden.

Period X.—97 years. Charles XII. of Sweden to fall of Napoleon.

Period XI.—40 years. Napoleon to the year 1850.

IMPORTANT EVENTS.

2347 B. C. Wine made by Noah from the grape.

2247. Bricks made and cement used to unite them. Confusion of languages at Babel.

2234. Astronomical observations begun at Babylon.

2100. Sculpture and painting employed to commemorate exploits of Osymandyas.

2095. Pyramids and canals in Egypt. The science of Geometry began to be cultivated.

1920. Gold and silver first mentioned as money.

1891. Letters first used in Egypt by Syphoas.

1822. Memnon invents the Egyptian alphabet.

B. C.
1588. Atlas, the astronomer, flourished.
1534. Dancing to music introduced by Curetes. Book of Job written about this time.
1506. The flute invented by Hyagnis, a Phrygian.
1921. Abraham called: goes into Egypt, 1920; delivers Lot from captivity and receives the blessing of Melchizedec, 1912; Ishmael born, 1909; Sodom and Gomorrah destroyed, 1897, also God renews his covenant with Abraham; Isaac born, 1896; Abraham commanded to offer Isaac in sacrifice, 1871.
1824. Abraham dies, 172 years old
1729. Joseph sold into Egypt.
1571. Moses born.
1491. The exodus of Israelites from Egypt.
1556. Athens founded by Cecrops.
1490. Crockery made by the Egyptians and Greeks.
1453. Olympic games first celebrated in Greece.
1284. Orpheus and Linus skilled in music.
1263. The Temple of Apollo at Delphi built.
1240. The axe, wedge, nimble and lever, also masts and sails for ships, invented by Dædalus of Athens.
1224. The game of backgammon invented by Palamedes of Greece.
1194. Trojan War begins.
1115. Mariner's Compass said to be known in China.
1124. Thebes founded.
1085. David born.
1004. Dedication of Solomon's Temple,
937. Breastplates invented by Jason.
886. Homer's poems brought into Greece.
800. Carpets in use for tents.
772. Scripture first mentioned in profane history.
680. Chess invented.
640. The spherical form of the Earth and the true course of lunar eclipses taught by Thales.
606. Sappho, Chilo, Æsop and Cadmus flourish.
599. Birth of Cyrus.
578. Money coined at Rome by Servius Tullius.
562. First comedy in Athens.
522. Confucius, the Chinese philosopher flourished.
559. Handwriting on the wall.
538. Babylon taken by Cyrus.
507. Heraclitus, Theano, Protagoras, Anaxagoras, philosopher, and Corinna, poetess, flourish.

B. C.
500. The Phœnician letters carried to Ireland from Spain. The Temple of Minerva built.
479. Æschylus flourished.
447. Thucydides born.
468. Sophocles, the tragic poet, and Plato, the comic, born.
490. Darius sends 500 men into Greece.
478. Death of Confucius.
450. The Britons inflict punishment of death by drowning in a quagmire.
441. The battering-ram invented by Artemones.
432. Socrates, the greatest of heathen moralists; Thucydides and Ctesias, historians, flourished.
410. Thucydides' history ends, and Xenophon's begins.
335. Alexander enters Jerusalem.
320. The first work on Mechanics. Diving-bell first mentioned.
312. The Appian Way constructed. The gnomon invented to measure altitudes.
300. Euclid of Alexander, the celebrated mathematician; Zeno, founder of the Stoics, and Epicurus, flourished. The great Chinese Wall built.
283. The Pharaohs build, at Alexandria, the first light-house.
264. The first Punic War.
224. Archimedes demonstrates the properties of the lever and other mechanical powers; constructs a planetarium.
219. The art of surgery introduced.
218. The second Punic War.
200. Jesus, the son of Sirach, writes Ecclesiasticus.
170. Paper invented in China. Jerusalem and the Temple plundered by Antiochus Epiphanes, who attempts to abolish the Jewish religion.
149. Third Punic War.
146. Alexandria the center of commerce.
113. First great migration of the German nations.
70. First water mill described.
63. Judea a Roman province.
60. Cicero, Sallust, Lucretius and Catullus, Aristomedes of Crete, the grammarian, flourished.
30. Egypt becomes a Roman province. Golden age of Roman literature.
29. Temple of Janus, at Rome, closed, there being a general peace.
19. The Temple rebuilt by Herod.

A. D.
4. Birth of Christ, four years before the Vulgar era.
26. John the Baptist begins his ministry.

A. D.
30. Crucifixion of our Saviour, Friday, April 3, 3 P. M. Resurrection, Sunday, April 5. Ascension, Thursday, May 4.
33. St. Peter baptizes Cornelius.
40. Disciples first called Christians.
64. Nero's golden palace built. First persecution of Christians, by Nero.
66. Pliny, the elder, author of the first natural history.
67. Josephus, the Jewish historian, flourished.
70. Destruction of Jerusalem by Titus.
79. Herculaneum and Pompeii destroyed by an irruption of Vesuvius.
95. Second persecution of the Christians, by Domitian. St. John writes his gospel.
96. Tacitus, historian, Juvenal, Plutarch and the younger Pliny flourished.
107. The first credible historian among the Chinese. Third persecution of Christians, by Trajan.
118. Fourth persecution of Christians, by Adrian.
183. The Jewish talmud and targum composed.
202. Fifth persecution of Christians, under Severus.
235. Sixth persecution of Christians, under Maximinus.
250. Seventh persecution of Christians.
272. Ninth persecution of Christians, under Aurelian.
303. Tenth persecution of Christians.
323. The foundation of Constantinople, by Constantine.
325. The Council of Nice, from June 19 to August 25, consisting of 318 bishops who condemn Arianism.
306. Constantine the Great, the first Christian Emperor.
373. The Bible translated into the Gothic language.
381. The second grand Council of Constantinople.
410. Rome sacked and burned by the Goths.
468. Oligarchy of the bishops of Rome, Constantinople, Alexandria, Antioch and Jerusalem, all striving for the supremacy. The Church now begins to assume a political aspect.
476. Rome taken by Odoacer, king of the Herulii. End of the Western Empire, 1228 years after the building of Rome.
486. Rise of the Feudal system in France, under Clovis.
494. The Roman Pontiff asserts his supremacy.
519. The orthodox bishops restored, by Justin.
526. Pope Felix IV.
558. Procopius, a Roman historian, the last of the classic writers.
569. The Turks first mentioned in history; they send embassies to Justin and form an alliance.

A. D.

568. The old Roman municipal system of Italy overthrown by the invasion of the Lombards, and the feudal system established. Written laws compiled among the nations of German origin, first by the Visigoths, in Spain. Semi-circular arches introduced in the architecture of churches.

580. The Latin language ceases to be spoken in Italy, while it supercedes the Gothic in Spain.

588. Gregory of Tours, the father of French history, flourished.

598. St. Augustine introduces Christianity into Britain.

607. Supremacy of the Pope acknowledged in Britain.

617. Ethelbert publishes the first code of laws in England.

610. Mahomet publishes a Koran.

625. Africa and Asia, with the Churches of Jerusalem, Alexandria and Antioch, lost to the Christian world by the progress of Mohammedanism.

636. Christianity introduced into China.

644. Celibacy of the clergy enjoined.

622. The Hegira or Mahomet's flight from Mecca to Medina.

632. Death of Mahomet.

674. Stone buildings, and glass, come into use in England.

676. The Popes become independent of the Greek Emperor.

711. The custom of kissing the Pope's foot introduced.

716. The art of making paper brought from Samarcand by the Arabs.

704. The first province given to the Pope.

720. Dark period of European literature.

727. Peter's pence first collected in England.

779. Imposition of tithes, enforced by Charlemagne, for the support of the clergy, churches, schools and the poor.

783. The first palm-tree planted in Spain.

785. Golden period of learning in Arabia.

787. The seventh general Council at Nice.

788. Pleadings in courts of justice first practiced.

787. Britain, first recorded invasion by the Danes.

800. The Pope separates from the Eastern Empire and becomes supreme Bishop of the Western.

800. New Empire of the West, founded by Charlemagne, who is crowned at Rome, by the Pope, King of Italy, Germany and France.

806. Charlemagne divides the Empire between his three sons.

817. The College of Cardinals founded.

844. The aristocratic feudal system in all its power; hereditary nobility, which, with the clergy, was the dominant order of the State.

849. Alfred the Great born.

A. D.
862. Russia—Ruric, first grand Prince, builds the city of Lagoda.
890. Oxford University founded. Alfred the Great establishes militia and navy, and the mode of trial by jury; institutes fairs and markets.
941. The figures of arithmetic brought into Europe by the Saracens.
982. Greenland discovered by the Norwegians.
993. First canonization of saints.
1002. Paper made of cotton rags. Churches first built in Gothic style. The French language first began to be written.
1024. Musical scale, consisting of six notes, invented by Guido Aretino.
1066. Feudal system introduced into England by the Normans.
1076. Booksellers first heard of.
1096. The first Crusade; Peter the Hermit and Walter the Pennyless set out with a vast rabble; 300,000 perish before the warriors are ready to start.
1147. The second Crusade.
1150. The magnetic needle known in Italy.
1178. The Waldenses spread over the valley of Piedmont.
1190. Third Crusade, led by Philip Augustus, of France. The Jews become the principal bankers of the world.
1200. The power of the Pope supreme, and kings obedient to his authority; the Pope excommunicates Philip of France.
1204. The Inquisition of France.
1209. The order of Franciscan Friars instituted.
1217. The fifth Crusade, by Andrew II., King of Hungary.
1229. The Scriptures forbidden to all laymen.
1233. First discovery of coal, at Newcastle.
1265. First regular Parliament in England.
1270. Prince Edward joins the eighth Crusade.
1274. Fourteenth general Council at Lyons; first re-union of the Eastern and Western Churches.
1296. The influence of the Crusades was great, expanding the mind of Europe, refining the general manners, exciting the spirit of geographical research and adventure, and promoting improvement in the arts and sciences.
1299. Foundation of the Ottoman or Turkish Empire in Bythinia, under Othman I.
1300. University of Lyons founded. Rapid advances in civilization. Improvements in arts and sciences.
1302. The mariner's compass invented at Naples, by Giora.
1323. John De Muris introduces notes of different length into music, and the method of distinguishing them.

A. D.
1340. Gunpowder in use at the battle of Cressy.
1492. Discovery of America.
1517. Luther, Erasmus, Melancthon and other reformers flourished. Copernicus discovers the true system of the universe. Commencement of the Reformation. America—First patent for importing negroes.
1522. First complete circum-navigation of the globe, by Magellan.
1521. Diet of Worms.
1539. Calvin founds the University of Geneva.
1538. Diving-bell invented. John Knox, Scottish reformer, flourished.
1545. Council of Trent.
1580. Tobacco first brought to Europe.
1588. First newspaper in England.
1590. Telescopes invented, by Jausen, a German.
1606. Dr. Gilbert discovers the power of electricity, and of conductors and non-conductors.
1618. Harvey discovers the circulation of the blood.
1603. James I. Union of the English and Scotch crowns.
1630. Lotteries for money first mentioned.
1639. First printing office in America, at Cambridge.
1654. Air pump invented.
1662. Logwood first cut in the bay of Honduras.
1666. Chain shot invented by De Witt.
1670. Bayonets invented by Bayonne.
1690. White paper first made in England.
1683. John Bunyan's "Pilgrims' Progress."
1692. Telescopes—First reflecting one on the principles of Sir Isaac Newton. Witchcraft superstition in New England. John Locke and Sir Isaac Newton flourished in England.
1693. Bank of England.
1699. Phosphorus discovered.
1701. Yale College founded.
1709. Prussic acid discovered by Diesbach.
1710. A Post-office in America at New York.
1716. The first standing army in England.
1717. New Orleans settled by the French.
1719. First Philadelphia newspaper.
1729. Balloons invented by Gusmac.
1733. First lodge of Free Masons at Boston.
1750. Dr. Franklin's discoveries in electricity.
1761. Potatoes first planted in France. Wesley and Whitfield preach.
1765. American Stamp Act resisted in Massachusetts. First Colonial Congress at New York.
1767. First spinning machine in England.

A. D.
1768. Cook's first voyage of discovery. Bruce discovers the source of the Nile.
1773. Tea destroyed at Boston.
1774. The spinning-jenny invented by Robert Arkwright; the improved steam engine by Watts and Bolton. Goldsmith, Warburton, Johnson, Littleton, Lowth, Garrick, Hume, Robertson, Blackstone, Adam Smith, Horne Tooke, Priestley, Horsley, Burke, Pitt, Fox, Cooper, Sheridan, McPherson, Burns, Kaimes and Reid flourished in England. Voltaire, Rousseau, Diderot, Condillac, Jessien, Lavoisier, La Harpe, Bartholemy and Buffoe flourished in France. Mosheim, Zimmerman, Kant, Klopstock, Lessing, Wieland, Herder, Goethe, Schiller, flourished in Germany. Linnæus flourished in Sweden. Metastasio flourished in Italy. Kheraskov, Kostrov, Deerhavin, Bogdanovitch, Khemitzee, flourished in Russia.
1775. American Revolution. Skirmish at Lexington, April 19. Battle of Bunker Hill, June 17.
1776. British troops evacuate Boston. July 4th, Declaration of Independence.
1777. Arrival of LaFayette.
1783. Independence of the United States acknowledged by Great Britain.
1784. First American vessel in China.
1787. General Convention at Philadelphia. Federal Constitution of the United States adopted.
1788. Cotton planted in Georgia.
1789. George Washington first President.
1791. First United States Bank.
1792. Kentucky admitted into the Union. United States Mint established.
1793. Washington re-elected.
1794. Commercial treaty with England. Commencement of the Navy; six frigates built.
1795. Napoleon Bonaparte commander of the French army.
1796. Washington resigns.
1797. John Adams second President. Bonaparte's Austrian campaign.
1798. Bonaparte's expedition to Egypt. Defeated by Nelson.
1800. Union of England and Ireland.
1801. Thomas Jefferson third President. Iron railways first laid in England.
1802. Ohio joins the Union; 76,000 inhabitants.
1803. Purchase of Louisiana for $15,000,000.
1805. Jefferson re-elected President.
1804. First locomotive steam engines on the Merthyr Tydvil road

A. D.

in Wales. Napoleon Bonaparte crowned as Napoleon I., Emperor of France.

1806. Planet Juno discovered.

1807. Fulton's first successful trial of steamboats. Bill for the abolition of the slave trade passed.

1808. Lithography invented.

1809. James Madison fourth President.

1810. First steamboat built in Europe.

1812. War with Great Britain. Invasion of Canada under Gen. Hull. Louisiana admitted into the Union. Russian Campaign. Moscow entered by Napoleon and burned.

1813. Perry's victory. Tecumseh killed.

1814. City of Washington burnt by the British. Steam carriages in England. Gas used for lighting the streets of London. Battle of Leipsic. Napoleon abdicates. House of Bourbon restored. Louis XVIII.

1815. Napoleon returns from Elba. The hundred days. Napoleon victorious at Ligny. Battle of Waterloo. The Allies enter Paris. Bonaparte banished to St. Helena.

1816. Indiana admitted.

1817. James Monroe elected fifth President. Public Schools established throughout Russia.

1819. First passage of the Atlantic by steam, by the Savannah, New York to Liverpool. The Republic of Colombia declared; Bolivar President.

1820. Maine admitted. George IV. king.

1821. Monroe re-elected. Missouri admitted. Slavery compromise. Death of Napoleon at St. Helena.

1822. Hieroglyphics deciphered by Champollion. Sir William Herschel died.

1824. Erie Canal opened. Protective tariff.

1825. J. Q. Adams sixth President. Steam navigation on the Rhine. Russia—Nicholas I. King.

1829. General Jackson seventh President. Captain Ross' voyage to discover the Northwest Passage. Pius VIII. Pope. Venezuela independent.

1831. The first newspaper in Constantinople.

1832. Cholera in New York. Trade Unions in France, Germany, Switzerland, &c. Nullification in South Carolina. Gen. Jackson's celebrated proclamation.

1833. Gen. Jackson re-elected to the Presidency. Girard College commenced. Spain—Isabella Queen. Removal of the deposits from the United States Bank.

A. D.
1834. Inquisition abolished in Spain.
1835. Great fire in New York. Slavery abolished in the British colonies.
1836. The National debt of the United States being paid, the surplus revenue is divided among the States.
1837. Victoria Queen. Martin Van Buren eighth President. The independence of Texas acknowledged. S. F. B. Morse takes out a patent for his electro-magnetic telegraph (invented, 1832.) Suspension of specie payments by the banks of the United States, in May.
1838. Talleyrand dies in France.
1839. The daguerreotype invented in Paris. Antarctic continent discovered by the United States exploring expedition. Peace between France and Mexico. China—The opium trade forbidden.
1840. Penny postage system in England.
1841. W. H. Harrison ninth President. He dies April 4th, one month after inauguration. John Tyler succeeded him as tenth President. Sub-Treasury Act repealed, August 9th.
1842. Treaty between United States and England, settling the northeastern boundary. The Croton Aqueduct in New York completed.
1843. Great Repeal agitation in Ireland.
1844. Texas annexed to the United States. Anti-Rent broached in State of New York.
1845. Treaty with China. James K. Polk eleventh President. Sir John Franklin sails in search of the North-west Passage. Gutta percha in use. Lord Rosse's telescope.
1846. War with Mexico. Hostilities commence on the Rio Grande, April 24. Battle Palo Alto, May 8; Resaca de la Palma, May 9. The Oregon Treaty with Great Britain, settling the north-western boundary, signed at London, June 18. Commodore Sloat takes possession of California, July 6. New Tariff bill passed, establishing *ad valorem* duties. Battle of Monterey, September 23. Tampico occupied, November 14.
1847. Battles Buena Vista, February 22; Sacramento, February 26. Vera Cruz surrenders, March 29. Battles Cerro Gordo, April 18; Contreras, August 20. Armistice, August 24. Hostilities renewed, September 7. Battles Molino del Rey, September 8; Chepultepec, September 12. Mexico surrenders, September 14.
1848. Treaty of peace with Mexico signed at Guadaloupe Hidalgo, February 22.
1848. Civil war in Ireland.
1849. Zachary Taylor twelfth President. Magnetic telegraph in the United States, 10,000 miles; railroads, 6,000 miles. Magnetic clock invented by Dr. Locke in Cincinnati.

A. D.

1850. Great agitation of the slavery question in United States. J. C. Calhoun died in Washington. Death of Gen. Taylor, July 9. Millard Fillmore thirteenth President. California admitted, 31st State. Texas boundary settled by the payment of $10,000,000 to Texas. New Mexico and Utah admitted as territories. Bill for the arrest of fugitive slaves passed by Congress. Slave trade in the District of Columbia abolished. Sir Robert Peel dies. Louis Phillippe dies in England. Disunion meetings held at Natchez (many present opposed to disunion). Union meetings in different cities.

1851. Erie railroad opened from New York city to Dunkirk, 469 miles. Nicaragua route between New York and San Francisco opened, August 12. Kossuth arrives in New York, December. Revolution of Louis Napoleon Bonaparte. He secures the reins of government. The election results in the confirmation of Bonaparte for President for ten years.

1852. Southern Rights Convention at Montgomery, Alabama. Henry Clay dies, June 29. Daniel Webster dies, October 24.

1853. Franklin Pierce declared elected President. Great heat throughout the country. A mob demolishes the railroad track near Erie, Pa., December 9.

1854. Commercial Treaty concluded between the United States and Japan.

1855. Panama Railroad completed. Suspension Bridge at Niagara Falls first crossed, March 14.

1856. N. P. Banks, of Massachusetts, elected Speaker of House of Representatives of United States, after a contest of nine weeks, by a plurality of three votes, February 2. Mr. Fillmore nominated for President by American Convention at Philadelphia, February 22. Personal assault on Senator Sumner, of Massachusetts, by Brooks, of South Carolina, May 22. John W. Geary confirmed as Governor of Kansas, July 31. James Buchanan elected President, November 4.

1857. The Dred Scott decision delivered by Chief Justice Taney, March 6. The Atlantic Cable first joined at sea by the Niagara and Agamemnon, August 5; breaks, August 11.

1857. "Lecompton Constitution" adopted by Convention, Nov. 9.

1858. New Prohibitory Liquor Law voted in Maine. News of the completion of the Atlantic telegraph, with joyful demonstrations, August 5. First overland mail for California leaves St. Louis, September 16. First railroad in Egypt.

1859. New Hall of the United States Senate first occupied, January 4. John Brown's raid for the liberation of slaves, at Harper's Ferry, Va., October 17; 12 of his men and one marine killed, two of his men hung, December 16, and two more, March 16, 1860.

A. D.

1860. National Democratic Convention (adjourned) at Baltimore, June 18, nominates Douglas and H. V. Johnson; a seceding Convention nominates Breckenridge and Lane. Dr. Hayes' Arctic expedition from Boston sails July 7. Visit of the Prince of Wales to British North America and the United States. Lincoln and Hamlin elected by the vote of all the Northern States, except New Jersey, which chose 4 electors for Douglas and 3 for Lincoln. This election is made the pretext for "rebellion and secession" of the Cotton States; South Carolina leading and adopting in Convention an ordinance of Secession from the United States, Dec. 20.

1861. This example followed by Mississippi, January 9; Alabama, January 11; Florida, January 12; Georgia, January 19; Louisiana, January 26. Attempt to carry Virginia, Kentucky, Tennessee, North Carolina, Missouri, and Arkansas for Secession defeated, January-March, 1861. Texas carried for Secession, but a strong re-action for Union follows. Gen. Twiggs surrenders the United States forces in Texas, and the military stores, to the State, Feb. Inauguration of Lincoln President, March 4. The Italian Parliament declares Victor Emanuel King of Italy, Feb.

1862. Monitor on trial trip commanded by Lieut. John L. Worden, March 9. Merrimac disabled. February 22, Jeff. Davis elected permanet President of the Confederacy, for a term of 6 years.

1863. Burnside superseded by Gen. Joseph Hooker, Jan 26. Gen. Meade assumed command when the army was lying at Frederick, Maryland, June 28.

1864. National forces in the field, 800,000; Confederates about half that number. Senate confirmed the nomination of U. S. Grant, Lieutenant-General, March 2; commissioned, March 8. Union National Convention, held at Baltimore, June 7. Mr. Lincoln nominated for President, and Andrew Johnson Vice-President. Democratic National Convention at Chicago nominated Geo. B. McClellan as President, and Geo. H. Pendleton as Vice-President, Aug. 28.

1865. April 14—President Lincoln, while seated in a private box of a theatre in Washington city, John Wilkes Booth crept behind him and shot him through the head with a pistol ball. Then leaping upon the stage with the cry of "*Sic semper tyrannis*"—the legend of Virginia's State seal—Booth turned to the audience, and brandishing a dagger, exclaimed, "*The South is avenged.*" Mr. Lincoln expired, April 15.

1866. President by proclamation declared the Civil War at an end, April 2.

1867. Nevada becomes the thirty-seventh State, over the President's veto.

1868. Feb. 22—The House of Representatives, by 126 to 47, "Resolved

A. D.

that Andrew Johnson, President of the United States, be impeached of high crimes and misdeamors." The Senate was organized as a jury for the trial of the President, Chief Justice Chase, presiding, March 5. On the 13th the President appeared at the bar, by his counsel, who asked for a space of 40 days to prepare an answer to the indictment. Ten days were granted, and on the 23d the President's counsel presented an answer. The Senate allowed seven days more, and on the 30th day of March the trial began. Examination of witnesses closed 22d of April. The arguments of counsel closed 6th of May. Its decision was given 25th of the same month. Every member of the Senate was present and voted. Thirty-five pronounced the President guilty, and nineteen not guilty; he escaped conviction by one vote. Public debt, $2,500,000,000.

1869. Gov. Hoffman inaugurated Governor. Com. Vanderbilt married, August 21. Death of Gen. Wool, Nov. 10. Unveiling of the Vanderbilt bronze, "Black Friday," Sept. 24. Opening of Ecumenical Council, Dec. 8. Death of Edward M. Stanton, Dec. 24.

1870. Completion of Brigham Young's railway, the Utah Central, Jan. 10. Death of Anson Burlingame at St. Petersburg, Feb. 23. President Grant proclaims the 15th amendment part of the Constitution, March 30. Ecumenical Council adopt a constitution of faith, April 24, Completion of Denver Pacific R. R., June 24. Isabella of Spain abdicates in favor of her son, June 26. Napoleon assumes command of the army. War between France and Prussia, July 30. Gen. Robert E. Lee died, Oct. 12. Rev. Albert Barnes died, Oct. 24.

1871. Theirs declared head of French Government, Feb. 17. Avery D. Putnam murdered by Foster, April 27. Goldsmith Maid trots 2:17 on Cold Spring track, Milwaukee, Sept. 7. W. M. Tweed arrested, Oct. 27. Richard B. Connolly arrested, Nov. 25. Grand Duke Alexis arrives in Buffalo, Dec. 23.

1872. Jas. Fisk, Jr., assassinated at Grand Central Hotel, Jan. 6. Lord Mayo, Governor General of India, assassinated Feb. 8. Greeley and Brown nominated at Cincinnati, May 3. Funeral of W. H. Seward at Auburn, New York, Oct. 10. Unusual prevalence of horse disease, Oct. Grant elected President; John A. Dix elected Governor of New York, Nov. 4. Horace Greeley died, Nov. 29; his body lies in state in New York, and is visited by 20,000 people, Dec. 2. James Gordon Bennett died aged 76, June 1.

1873. Ex-Emperor Napoleon dies at Chiselhurst, England, Jan. 9. Trial of W. M. Tweed, Jan. 14. Roscoe Conkling re-elected to United States Senate, Jan. 22. King Amadeus abdicates the Spanish throne, Feb. 10. Gen. Grant inaugurated President, March 4. Steamer Atlantic wrecked, April 1. Capt. Jack and the Modocs convicted of murder,

UNIVERSAL HISTORY.

July 30. Kenyon, Cox & Co. failed. *Graphic* balloon bursts, Sept. 12 J. Cooke & Co., great bankers, fail, and creates a general panic, Sept. 18. Great panic in New York city, Sept. 19. The financial panic reaches its height in Chicago, Sept. 22. Meeting of Evangelical Alliance opens in New York, Oct. 3. Trial of Marshal Bazaine, Oct. 6. Firm of A. & W. Sprague, of Providence, R. I., fails, Oct. 30. W. M. Tweed found guilty; sentenced to 12 years' imprisonment and a fine of $12,700, Nov. 19. French steamer Ville du Havre sunk at sea by Lochearn; 226 lives lost, Nov. 22. Prof. Agassiz dies, Dec. 12.

1874. The late panic of 1873 seriously affects the business prosperity for 1874. Congress—Discussion of the currency question; inflation and contraction about equal. Temperance crusades; organizing of ladies' praying circles, visiting saloons and praying for proprietors. Gladstone defeated; Disraeli forms a new ministry, Feb. Judge N. K. Hall of Buffalo died, March 2. Ex-President Millard Fillmore died at Buffalo, March 8; buried, March 12, with imposing ceremonies. Hon. Charles Sumner died, March 11.

PUBLISHING AND ADVERTISING HOUSE,

Established 1860, in Buffalo, N. Y.

W. T. HORNER, A. M., Proprietor,

EDITOR OF THE TEMPERANCE JOURNAL, THE RAILWAY GUIDE, THE ENCYCLOPEDIA OF USEFUL KNOWLEDGE, AND GUIDE TO NIAGARA FALLS, FOR THE PRINCIPAL CITIES OF THE UNITED STATES.

Our system of general advertising reaches every State and Territory of this country. A general agent established in each State.

LOCAL ADVERTISING MEDIUMS,
The Largest and Best.

EVERY EDITION GUARANTEED.

The Printing Department embraces

Books, Pamphlets & Lithography,

and every kind of

PLAIN AND ORNAMENTAL PRINTING,

ENGRAVING ON WOOD OR STONE,

In style unsurpassed by any establishment in the United States, and at rates defying competition. Good canvassing agents wanted. Address
W. T. HORNER, BUFFALO, N. Y.

INDEX.

BUFFALO.	Page.
Almshouse	17
Amusement, Places of	21
American Block	29
Banks	49
Cattle Yards	31
Charitable Institutions	11
Churches	39, 41
City and County Hall	15
Elevators	31
Fire Department	21
Forest Lawn Cemetery	19
Hospital, Buffalo General	19
Insane Asylum	15
International Bridge	25
Jail	19
Manufacturing Establish'ts	31, 35
Military	21
Newspapers, etc	41, 43
Parks	7
Penitentiary	19
Police Force	19
Port of Buffalo	5
Public Offices	49
Public Schools	9
Railroad Depots	25
Secret Societies	43, 45, 47
Societies, Libraries, etc	11, 13
Sporting Memoranda	51, 53
Street Cars	25
Water Works	17
Buff., N. Y. & Phila. R. R	42
Mich. Cen. & Great Western	42
Directory	54 to 63

NIAGARA FALLS.

General Description	63 86

ENCYCLOPEDIA.

Battles of the Rebellion	106 to 108
Census Returns	100, 108
Distances from Washington	93
Lofty Structures	90
Money Order Rates	90
Mottoes of States	96
Popular Names of States and Cities	97
Population of United States and Foreign Cities	98, 99
Presidential Votes	94, 95
Railway Construction	91, 92
Religious Denominations	101 to 104
Universal History	114 to 127
Useful Memoranda	109 to 113
Weights and Measures	105
World's Products	105

ADVERTISEMENTS.	Page.
Pierce's Family Medicines	4
Gowans & Co	6
Penrhyn Slate Co	8
E. D. Holman	8
S. D. Sikes & Bro	10
Joseph Churchyard	10
Eagle Iron Works	12
Brown & McCutcheon	12
Thebaud Bros	14
George E. Newman	14
Barnes, Bancroft & Co	16
Sibley & Holmwood	18
Wm. Wright	18
W. B. Sirret & Co	20
Sweet, Cook & Co	20
F. S. Pease	22
John D. Smith & Co	24
J. S Lytle & Son	24
Adam & Meldrum	26
Singer Sewing Machine	28
Bickford, Curtiss & Deming	30
Pratt & Letchworth	32
National Flour Mills	34
Fox & Williams	36
Booth, Riester & Co	36
John C. Post	36
M. W. Chase	38
J. L. Alberger & Co	38
Isaac D. White	38
Porter & Watkins	40
John Galt	40
Bergtold & Bro	44
R. Ovens & Son	46
Union Iron Co	48
Albert Best & Co	48
Tifft House	50
Hall & Sons	50
Allen Church	52
J. B. Pierce	34, 52
Drullard & Hayes	64
Farrar & Trefts	64
Kellogg Bridge Co	66
Clarke, Holland & Co	68
Wm. Woltge	70
Eagle File Works	70
T. Towers	70
DeWitt C. Weed	72
Lake Shore & Mich. So. R. R.	74
Toledo, Wabash & West'n R'y	74
Sidney Shepard & Co	79
Cornell Lead Co	83
J. O. Robson & Co	85
Guiteau & Hodge	85
D. B. Castle	87
Oriental Powder Mills	87
Bidwell's Livery Stable	87

www.ingramcontent.com/pod-product-compliance
Lightning Source LLC
Chambersburg PA
CBHW020112170426
43199CB00009B/496